To. Barry.
Christmas 1989
with love from
Wendy

FISHING TACKLE
FOR
COLLECTORS

CHARLES KEWLEY & HOWARD FARRAR

FISHING TACKLE
FOR
COLLECTORS

SOTHEBY'S PUBLICATIONS

© Elgin Press Limited 1987
© text Charles Kewley and Howard Farrar

This book designed and produced by
Elgin Press Limited
TR House, Christopher Road,
East Grinstead, Sussex RH19 3BT

First published 1987 for Sotheby's Publications by
Philip Wilson Publishers Limited
26 Litchfield Street
London WC2H 9NJ

and in the USA and Canada by
Sotheby's Publications
Harper & Row Publishers, Inc
10 East 53rd Street
New York
NY 10022

ISBN 0 85667 329 3
Library of Congress Catalog Number 87—060455

Printed in England by Springbourne Press Limited, Essex

Contents

List of colour plates 6

Foreword 7

Acknowledgements 8

Bibliography 8

Introduction 9

Rods 15

British reels 37

American reels 61

Flies and related equipment 73

Accessories 89

Hardy's of Alnwick 111

Manufacturers and their catalogues 128

The artistic angle 137

Appendix I 151

Appendix II 156

Index 158

List of colour plates

I ARTHUR FITZWILLIAM TAIT: Bass fishing.

II *A valise rod by William Blacker, c1850; a spike winch made by Long of Dublin, c1800; a leather pot-bellied creel by N. Thompson, c1780; a brass and steel gut line twister and turned wooden priest.*

III *A nineteenth-century trout rod with brass crank-handled reel by Farlows, a painted wooden creel and an ash-framed landing net with brass fittings.*

IV *The legendary Allcock's Ariel reel.*

V *A collection of nineteenth-century reels by Vom Hofe.*

VI *A Heddon multiplying reel, carrying the Carter's patent.*

VII *A collection of nineteenth-century tackle.*

VIII *Bait tins, a worm box and a gentle shute.*

IX *A small part of the Marchant Lane collection.*

X *A collection of antique accessories, including gaffs, floats and lures.*

XI *A very rare collection of nineteenth-century Hardy reels.*

XII *An 1891 patent 2$\frac{1}{2}$in. Hardy 'Perfect' fly reel.*

XIII *A 4$\frac{1}{2}$in. Hardy 'Hercules' reel.*

XIV *A Hardy copper cast box and salmon flies.*

XV HENRY ALKEN SNR.: On the Avon at Fordingbridge, 6$\frac{1}{2} \times 8\frac{3}{4}$in.

XVI JOHN RUSSELL: Still life with salmon and terrier.

Foreword

INTEREST in old fishing tackle has greatly increased during the last few years. This interest has led to more people collecting the tackle from the past. Some specialize in fly reels, others in spinning reels or miscellaneous piscatorial paraphernalia. Fewer, however, collect fishing rods, although there is a demand for knowledge as to when certain rods were manufactured. Perhaps they have less appeal than the smaller items because rods are more difficult to display, and many look much alike, the only real difference being in the balance in the hand. Certainly, with few exceptions, rods have never realized the same prices at auction as reels and sundry items: at a recent sale conducted by Sotheby's, over £4,000 was paid for an old Hardy reel.

Fishing tackle museums have been established, particularly in the United States, where the development of tackle can be seen. The House of Hardy is opening such a museum at their Alnwick factory in the near future. There, items from the full range of tackle manufactured since the formation of the company in 1872, will be on display.

There is little new in the way of original design today, and most developments during the past 25 years have been in raw materials. Those from which rods are made have gone through remarkable changes. During the nineteenth century, rods were constructed from lancewood, hickory, greenheart, single-built bamboo, double-built bamboo with steel centre and hollow steel tubing. This century has seen hollow-built bamboo, solid glass, glass-fibre tubing, carbon-fibre, boron and kevlar. The greatest advantage in all these changes of material has been lightness.

The patents taken out on all types of fishing reels are legion and have advanced the methods of angling through many stages. The improvements in spinning and bait-casting reels have been most significant and especially so in the case of big game fishing reels. Modern fishing line, whether for fly or bait fishing, has gone from natural materials, such as silk-worm gut and horsehair, to modern plastics. Flies and baits have advanced in both materials and design, but whether they catch more fish than in former years is a moot point.

This book describes and illustrates vintage fishing tackle and will, I am sure, be of the greatest interest to all devotees of the angle.

JAMES LEIGHTON HARDY
6th June 1987

Acknowledgements

Projects of this kind depend upon the generosity of many people and the authors are greatly indebted to other members of the angling fraternity, and to the following for the provision of photographs:

Sotheby's Sporting Guns Department
Christie's Scotland and Christie's New York
Bonham's, London
Philips, London and Exeter
Arthur Ackermann & Sons Ltd of Old Bond Street, London
The American Museum of Fly Fishing, Manchester, Vermont
Nicky Gibbs for the cover illustrations
Turrell Flies for the loan of research material
Nick Marchant Lane for the use of his collection

The authors wish to acknowledge a special debt to James Booth, Sotheby's specialist in sporting guns and equipment, for his invaluable help and advice, and for the provision of many photographs from the Sotheby's archives. James Hardy for his generous help in giving access to Hardy Brothers' archives. Robin Armstrong, whose second book linking fishing and painting is due to be published in Spring 1988, supplied all the colour photographs of Nick Marchant Lane's collection; the authors would like to thank them all for their generous help. Finally they are grateful to Frank Herrmann, without whose encouragement this book may never have begun.

Bibliography

DAME JULIANA BERNERS	*The Treatyse of Fysshyge with an Angle*, from *The Boke of St Albans*.
IZAAC WALTON	*The Compleat Angler*.
JOHN HARRINGTON KEENE	*Fishing Tackle, Its Materials and Manufacture*, Ward Locke 1886.
JOHN BICKERDYKE	*Sea Fishing*, Badminton Library, Longmans, Green & Co 1895.
H. CHOLMONDELEY-PENNELL	*Fishing (Salmon and Trout)* Badminton Library, Longmans, Green & Co 1893.
DANIEL	*Rural Sports*, London 1807.
R.B. MARSTON	*Fishing Gazette*, published weekly from 1877.
HARDY BROTHERS	*Anglers' Guide*, published annually
S. ALLCOCK & CO	*Anglers' Guide*, published annually
FOSTER BROTHERS	*Anglers' Guide*, published annually
P.D. MALLOCH	*Fishing Tackle*, published annually
WILLIAM MILLS & SON	*Fishing Tackle*, published annually
A. CARTER & CO. LTD	*Rod, Line and Bait*, published annually
W.J. CUMMINS	*Fishing and Fishing Tackle*, published annually

Introduction

Angling is often claimed to be one of the most practised sports. This must be largely because, unlike most other sports, angling can be enjoyed by almost anyone. There are practically no restrictions as to age, sex or income bracket, and few as to locality, provided some water is available.

The repertoire of angling literature contains abundant evidence of the sport's appeal to women over the centuries. There are numerous engravings of the eighteenth century which depict women angling, although quite how seriously is in some doubt. Few girls have passed through childhood with no angling experience at all. Big game fishing, largely a twentieth-century development of the sport, may be available only to an affluent few, but the majority of anglers enjoy the sport with whatever equipment they are able to afford, however rudimentary.

There are few sports, however, in which the combination of equipment is considered to be as important to the sportsman as it is in angling. Assembling the most appropriate rod, reel and bait for the particular conditions likely to prevail is an essential part of the angler's skill. It always has been. Old angling texts are full of advice about choosing the best tackle available, or the best materials for its construction. But apart from the introduction of the reel, or 'wynch' as it was originally termed in the seventeenth century, fishing tackle had remained virtually unchanged in centuries.

Rod making and fly tying were ancient and traditional crafts, using local materials to suit local conditions. Methods of manufacture and distribution were equally traditional. For centuries independent makers, skilled in light engineering, worked in numerous small 'shops', supplying either their own customers directly, or making reels to order for the tackle retailers. The old 'cottage industry' methods continued to be employed until they could no longer cope with demand and mass-production. The triumph of the industrial revolution, rendered them obsolete.

From the late seventeenth century there are numerous indications of close connections between horology and reel making. Some watch and clockmakers in both Britain and America also made fishing reels, and a number of noted reel makers were first apprenticed to horologists. This would be entirely logical as clockmakers already had the necessary skills in small-scale precision engineering and would have been able to adapt easily to reel making.

Fishing tackle was of the simplest construction and technical developments were few and far between until the surge of nineteenth-century inventiveness penetrated what had previously been a backwater. Then, what began as a trickle of improvements in the mid century, quickly swelled into a torrent by the end of it. The increasing affluence of the middle classes at that time brought with it the consequent luxury of leisure and the sport grew rapidly in popularity.

The 1870s opened a period of great innovation in both mechanics and materials. No longer were anglers prepared to tolerate shortcomings or limitations in their tackle. Solutions had to be found. Tackle manufacturers, as well as developing their own ideas, were prepared to work in conjunction with inventive anglers and often the results bore their joint names.

R.B. Marston, celebrated as an angler and as editor of the respected magazine *Fishing Gazette* had his reporters keep a watchful eye on the patents lodged at the Patent Office in order to be able to report the latest develpments to his readers. Contemporary accounts of what we now know as classic rods and reels make fascinating reading, as do the accounts of some of the more abstruse flights of fancy which never saw the light of day.

The public were quite as keen to see the latest innovations as they were to read about them. These were the great days of the trade exhibitions which followed the enormous success of the Great Exhibition of 1851. Huge crowds flocked, first to the Aquarium and later to the Crystal Palace, to see for themselves what had recently become available. The range was enormous, and as the tackle industry boomed the major manufacturers built and rebuilt their factories and became major employers. Much of the work still had to be carried out by hand, a type of work which especially suited female labour. Late nineteenth-century photographs of the Slater factory, typical of the leading manufacturers in both Britain and America, show hundreds of women seated at work-benches in human assembly lines, while the men carried out the more strenuous tasks. The large factories have now gone, not because there is no longer the same demand, but because the processes have at last become mechanized.

The second half of the nineteenth century also saw another revolution in the sport, that of dress. Unlike hunters in the field, anglers had never developed an appropriate costume. It seems somewhat surprising that anglers were content to set out, in any weather conditions, to muddy river banks or small boats, dressed for a gentle stroll in the park. Eighteenth and early nineteenth century prints show gentlemen in top

A very rare 3 in., 1891 pattern 'Perfect' trout reel. This particular reel belonged to Mr W.R. Hardy, the grandfather of the founder of the Hardy company, Mr J.L. Hardy.

hats and frock coats and ladies in large straw hats, printed gowns and dainty shoes. Could they be merely fair weather anglers? Surely not! It was probably because, until the mid-nineteenth century, the accoutrements of domestic life were relatively simple. It was the Victorians who, in the pursuit of ever greater gentility, invented many things no one had previously thought necessary. For a society which needed a different eating implement for almost every conceivable type of food, an appropriate costume for every activity was essential. Caps, sou'-westers, tweeds, plus-fours, macintoshes, specially warm underwear and waders all entered the well-stocked wardrobe, and have remained more or less unchanged to the present day.

Although the modern tackle industry has a relatively short history, surprisingly little of it is known. The history of manufacturing in general includes many instances of a complete lack of interest in keeping records of products once the market for them has ceased. The fishing tackle industry has proved to be no exception. It is not until a new market develops for the old products that there is suddenly a need to fill in the gaps in our knowledge. The market in old tackle is now flourishing and with it has come an interest in the history of the sport as a whole.

Anglers are not alone among sportsmen and women in taking an interest in the origins of their sport. The history of shooting and the demand for both antique and modern sporting guns are, of course, well established. In recent years

THEODORE LANE (*after*): The Enthusiast. *An engraving by Robert Graves, c.1820.*

golf and cricket have become the subjects of great interest and research, while the memorabilia and equipment of the sports rise rapidly in demand and price. One of the features of the second half of the twentieth century has been an intensifying wave of nostalgia, as the pace of scientific and technological development increases. Antiques of all descriptions have become so fashionable and highly priced that collectors are now looking to items uncomfortably close to the memories of those of us who regard the sixties 'as but yesterday'.

Research into the history of angling and the fishing tackle industry has only just begun, and is fraught with difficulties. The very early years are shrouded in obscurity and seem beyond recall, while the surge in popularity of the sport towards the end of the nineteenth century produced such a plethora of equipment and advice that many books will be required to cover them adequately. It is surprising that, in spite of so much activity in the tackle industry in the past century, so little of it should have been adequately recorded. The neglect of recent decades has resulted in the loss of much valuable material. In all too many cases company records have failed to survive takeovers, the devastation of war, or the lack of interest in discontinued products. Few of the individual makers have left any records at all and most of what we know of them is to be gleaned from contemporary references.

Fishing tackle prior to the mid-nineteenth century will be of only academic interest to most collectors. Little of it has survived and much of that is difficult to date with accuracy as methods and materials changed little in many decades. The items which will appeal to most collectors come from the great period of tackle development, about 1870 to 1930. As Mr James Hardy has commented in his Foreword, there has been little change except in materials since that time.

The market in old tackle is a thing of very recent times, although a few notable collections have been formed in the past. But already auctions, some wholly devoted to tackle and others including it among other sporting items, are now a regular feature. Prices are rising, steadily in most cases and rapidly in others. So far the main area of interest has centred on the reel and less on the rod, probably for practical reasons of storage and display. Some of the more decorative accessories are also becoming popular, especially in the United States, where the desirable hand-carved bass plugs can make large sums. Recent though the collecting interest has been, many of the rarer items are already in short supply.

A stuffed pike by J. Cooper & Sons, London. They were amongst the most famous of taxidermists, and were the only company to work exclusively with fish.

A: *a small bellied live bait can, for transporting small fish which were used for bait in pike fishing.* **B:** *a live bait horn for carrying worms, gentles and sometimes flies.* **C:** *a brass hinged and hatched clearing ring, from the late 1800s.* **D:** *a mid nineteenth-century red and black turned wooden priest, the head of which has been weighted with lead.* **E:** *a multiplying pole winch of brass with a collar foot, still retaining the leather pad.*

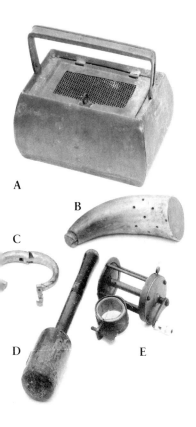

Only a few years ago a dealer considered himself fortunate to obtain five shillings for a large big-game reel, and then the demand might, very likely, come from a small boy eager to have a winch for his kite.

Natural wastage is, of course, quite normal and adds to the rarity of many items and, consequently, to the value of what remains. But there are also many instances where rarity was inbuilt from the start. Certain models of both rod and reel were in production for a very limited period, either to preserve their exclusivity for a special customer, or because they failed to find a market. Such an instance might be found in the Hardy White-Wickham reel. Although this reel appeared in the catalogue between 1934 and 1939, research into the Hardy Production Book for the period reveals that only two examples were actually made! The authors are grateful to Mr James Hardy for permission to reproduce those parts of the Production Book which have survived. It contains valuable information on the precise quantities of rods and reels produced in the period covered.

Certain items of old tackle appeal to one group of angler collectors as much for use as for historical interest or investment. For these collectors, their favourite items of old tackle are superior to anything which has superseded them. American buyers, especially, favour the early shorter length Hardy split-cane rods for present-day fly fishing. It is surely a testament to the fine craftsmanship of the manufacturers that these items are still capable of giving service in what can be far from a gentle sport. Unfortunately for these collectors they must now compete in a rising market.

Since Izaac Walton penned his classic work *The Compleat Angler* in the seventeenth century, a very considerable body of literature on angling has built up. Every conceivable aspect of the sport has been covered, including practical advice on the methods of making and using one's tackle, scientific studies of fish — often beautifully illustrated — and any number of personal accounts of fishing by anglers themselves. However, they have had little time in which to use up much ink on the latest facet of the sport, that of collecting old tackle.

This book does not attempt to take on the impossible task of covering the vast subject in detail. It seeks to sketch a picture of the historical background to the major technical developments of an industry which now supplies millions of anglers all over the world.

A

B

C

D   E

CHAPTER ONE

Rods

A PARTY ANGLING.

GEORGE MORLAND (*after*): A Party Angling. *A mezzotint by George Keeting and William Ward, published in 1789. Note the sectional poles being used and the absence of winches, which were available during this period.*

RODS of the seventeenth and eighteenth centuries were invariably of one piece with the line fixed to the top. The length of the rod varied according to the width of water to be fished, and since these rods might be of 15 to 18 feet in length, they were clearly not easy to transport. No doubt many practical anglers made their own rods of local materials, such as ash and hazel. By the end of the seventeenth century, a flourishing rod-making industry was well established with such firms as Eaton and Deller

15

commencing business around 1680 in London and producing very elegant rods. Sad to say, very few of these early examples have survived.

A writer of the late eighteenth century, commenting on one of his seventeenth-century ancestors who was a keen angler, describes him as wearing 'His Fishing Coat, which, if not black, was at least of a very dark colour; a black velvet Cap, like those which Jockeys now wear, only larger; and a Rod with a stock as long as a Halbert'. He goes on to say how conspicuous this gentleman must have appeared to the neighbourhood – and somewhat sinister, all in black. Izaac Walton also describes anglers dressed in black, complete with black puritan hats. Conspicuous they may have appeared to the neighbours but it was exactly the opposite effect they intended to have on the fish. The writer explains that 'In these latter days, bag-rods have been invented, which the Angler may easily convey, so as not to proclaim to every one he meets where he is going.'.

The first sectional rods were produced in the late eighteenth century for the art of float fishing – with a bait, be it maggot, worm or bread. Sectional rods for fly fishermen quickly followed.

A writer in Daniel's *Rural Sports*, published in 1807, suggests that woods for rod making be cut at Christmas and left in the open for a year to season. Hazel was the most popular wood used and of all the varieties the cob-nut was the most favoured, as it produced the longest and straightest shoots. The hazel was also in plentiful supply, being widely used on farms for fencing, sheep hurdles and kindling. A hazel coppice would be trimmed and cut every five to seven years. From the trimmings would be selected the most suitable lengths of approximately one inch diameter; knots

The Hardy patent 'Lock-Fast' joint developed in the late nineteenth century, and of which they claimed; ... 'it is not possible to break by angling'.

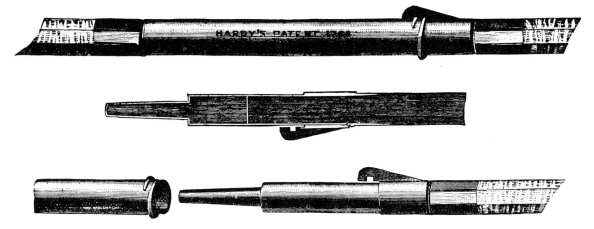

I ARTHUR FITZWILLIAM TAIT: Bass fishing.

II *A valise rod by William Blacker, c1850; a spike winch made by Long of Dublin, c1800; a leather pot-bellied creel by N. Thompson, c1780; a brass and steel gut line twister and turned wooden priest.*

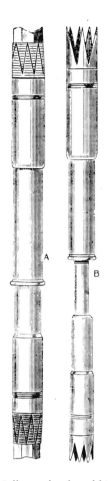

were avoided as these would weaken the rod. The tip section was made from rush ground shoots from the same plant which were of a tapered form. Any twigs were cut off, but not too close, to avoid damaging the bark which would affect the seasoning process and ultimately weaken the rod.

The selected shoots were kept dry until the following autumn, ready to be made into rods for the coming season. The process began by gently warming the shoots in front of a fire and setting them aside for a few days in as straight a position as possible. They were rubbed over with a piece of flannel soaked in linseed oil to remove excess bark and to polish them. They were then bound to a straight piece of wood and stored until the following spring. Some makers extended the seasoning process for as long as eighteen months to two years.

When the shoots were seasoned to the maker's satisfaction they were carefully matched to obtain the best taper for a two-, three- or even five-section rod. The length was determined by the width of water to be fished or, to some extent, by the angler's preference for the action of a long or short rod.

The quality of the joints was crucial to the action of the rod. However many sections were used the action had to be as one piece of wood. The two basic methods of joining the sections were:

Mr F. Malleson developed his 'New Safety Ferrule' in the late nineteenth century and in Keene's opinion it even surpassed those fitted to the Leonard rods. In Britain Malleson's rods were available through Bartleet & Sons of Redditch.

(*i*) with ferrules – hollow metal tubes forming a link between the sections.

(*ii*) with spliced joints – the adjoining ends of each section were cut to ensure that they sat closely upon each other and were then whipped together with leather thongs.

Spliced joints are still made by companies such as Sharp's of Aberdeen, renowned for retaining the craft for those anglers who feel that this method produces the most positive action. Sectional rods were of great benefit to anglers who had to travel to find the best waters. Spliced rods were also sectioned but more complicated to dismantle. Anglers who had no need to travel might therefore leave their spliced rods assembled for the whole season.

Rods at this early date were frequently varnished, using a mixture of linseed oil and India rubber, stirred slowly over a fire and applied to the rods to keep them dry and prevent warping. The flexible nature of this varnish was especially important for fly fishing rods, where the angler constantly flexes the rod while casting the line.

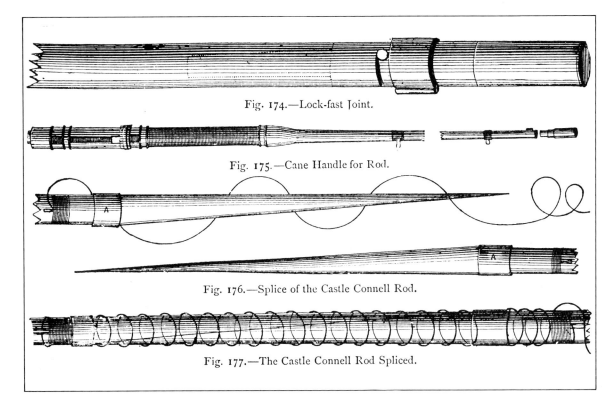

Fig. 174.—Lock-fast Joint.

Fig. 175.—Cane Handle for Rod.

Fig. 176.—Splice of the Castle Connell Rod.

Fig. 177.—The Castle Connell Rod Spliced.

While hazel was the most popular wood used in rod construction it was by no means the only one. In the early nineteenth century ash was considered to be the most suitable for salmon rods, because of its comparatively light weight. Lightness was an important consideration for a rod which might be used for casting over a wide river for the entire day. A salmon rod might extend to eighteen feet and was used with both hands on the stock (butt), whereas the shorter trout rod was cast with a single hand. Other woods mentioned by authors as being in common use during the eighteenth and nineteenth centuries were all native to Britain and included elder, holly, yew, mountain ash and hip briar.

A writer in Daniel's *Rural Sports* of 1807 describes the appropriate qualities and materials of rods for the various sporting fish:

The Angler should proportion the Length and Strength of his rods to the different fish; but they ought to bend regularly, taper gradually, be light in hand, and spring from the But end to the top, and recover their shape after being incurvated by the exertions of a large fish, which they will do if the materials are good: the great defect in

There were a number of different methods employed by rod-makers for connecting the rod sections. The diagram shows the three most common at the turn of the twentieth century.

most rods is, that the play is in the middle, owing to that part being too weak, where it bends like a waggon whip; with a rod of this kind, it is impossible to strike or command a fish of any size. For *Pike* and *Barbell*, sixteen feet is a proper length; the But ends of the rod may be made of *red deal*, the middle of *Ash*, and the tops (which may be shorter than the other joints) of *Hazel*; for Perch, Chub, Bream, Carp, Eels, Tench, the length may be shortenend and size reduced; small rings neatly whipped on for the line to run through, enable you to fish under bushes, and from eminences by the water, and likewise strengthen the rod in its smaller parts. For Roach, Dace, Gudgeons, Ruff, Bleak, eight or ten feet is quite sufficient, and the tops cannot be too elastic: . . .

The writer goes on to specify the requirements of a trout rod, which traditionally consisted of a But (or butt) end of yellow deal, seven feet long, then a straight section of hazel about six feet long, followed by a 'delicate piece of fine grained Yew, exactly tapered, and ending in a point of whalebone, both making about two feet'. A protective coloured varnish was then applied to the rod and a recommended recipe followed:

. . . to colour the stock, a feather dipped in *aqua fortis*, and rubbed into the deal, will give it a cinnamon colour; for a nut-brown colour, a quartern of spirit lacquer, half an ounce of Gamboge, the like quantities of Gum Sandrich and Dragon's blood; the last three to be powdered very fine, and as much of each of them as will lie upon a sixpence put into the spirit lacquer, which must be kept stirring, until properly mixed; the vial must be warmed as well as the wood, and the mixture gradually laid on with a Camel's hair brush; after it is dried, a second and third coat are to be applied: to make the colour redder, put double the quantity of Dragon's blood: to make the rod *mottled*, get green Copperas and dissolve in spring water; dip a linen tape in the liquid, and while wet twist it round about, and let it remain on the rod eight or ten hours in the cool; unbind the tape, which will be dry, and use the above-mentioned Varnish, which will give the desired effect. The Varnish also preserves the rings and the bindings that fix them to the rod. To fasten a fly rod of the above make properly, a piece of Shoemakers' wax was rubbed upon each splice; a handle of a knife, or any hard thing, was rubbed over them, until they were smooth; they were then tied neatly together, and were as firm as any part of the rod.

It is interesting to note how technical the manufacture of rods had become by the beginning of the nineteenth century and how well the properties of the 'ideal' rod were understood from this period. Rods were being made for specific types of fish, using the right woods and materials to suit different circumstances and the species of fish the angler would find in his locality. The well-defined degrees of strength, stiffness and elasticity of different tips and top sections of rods used for fishing carp, tench, perch, dace and roach, indicates that, apart from the introduction of split-bamboo rods, few essential changes were made in rod construction until the introduction of such modern materials as fibreglass, carbon-fibre and boron.

Split-cane rods were constructed in a number of different ways. The six-piece (LEFT) was a very common form, but in the late 1880s Hardy's produced a double-built steel-centred rod with twelve sections (BELOW).

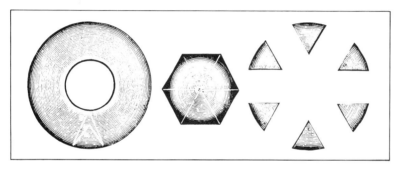

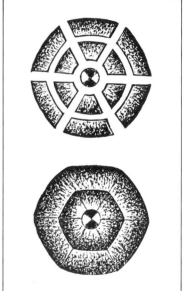

A common feature on a number of early rods was the hollowing of the butt end to store a variety of tops for the rod. This allowed the angler a choice of length and strength of top to suit his particular method of fishing. Tops were made of a springy material such as whalebone or, especially in Scotland, of tortoiseshell, which was considered to be lighter and springier than whalebone. They were very delicate and susceptible to damage and it was therefore sensible to carry a variety of spares especially in remote areas where repairs were difficult to make. The hollow butt was still a feature of fly rods at the end of the nineteenth century when all sectional rods were supplied with a carrying bag. By that time many rods were made to be entirely self-contained within the butt section. Late eighteenth-century rods are also occasionally found fitted with a spike to the butt. This enabled the angler to secure the rod in the ground, either while taking a rest or changing a fly. He might also use this device, having played a fish out and tired it, to fix the rod upright and keep a tight line while he moved downstream with his landing net. The spike continued to be in demand with some anglers until comparatively recently. Hardy's produced a rod with an aluminium spike until the late 1950s.

This rod is typical of the mid to late Victorian period, complete with its detachable brass spear. The reel is a brass crank handled fly reel, bearing the inscription 'John Osborn Norwich 1876' and is a typical example of a fly reel of the period, although the majority carry no inscription at all. The inscription on this reel may not bear any relation to the maker; it was probably a presentation reel. However, it does illustrate how confusing names and dates on early tackle can be.

With the introduction of the winch or reel in the eighteenth century, it became necessary to fit rings to rods to conduct the line to the tip. Where these have survived they appear to be of a fairly crude manufacture: a simple metal ring whipped to the rod. Contemporary writers recommend that a piece of quill also be whipped to the top ring to prevent the line from being cut when taking the strain of a large fish.

The complete salmon rod, as it appeared in 1807, is described in Daniel's *Rural Sports*:

The *rod* should not be less than *fifteen* feet, longer according to the breadth of the river, limber [easily flexible] yet strong, with wire rings, from the top to within three feet where the *Reel* is fixed, with a good *running-line*, without *knots*, made of either *silk* or *hair*, (the former is to be preferred,) and the *reel* must be large enough to contain four score yards, or at least as much as will reach more than *across* the river fished in. Wherever the *running-line* is directed, the *reel* is proper to be used; they are of various sizes, and may be proportioned to the coarseness or fineness of the *line*. The being enabled to give the *Salmon*, when hooked, plenty of line, is of great advantage to the Angler; for the fish will at first run swiftly, and afterwards leap and plunge, so that he must be humoured, and the line slacked and wound up again with great skill, until he is quite subdued, when he may be led to some shallow, where on his belly, touching the bottom, he will turn on his side, and be so jaded, that he may be taken out by the gills.

(*Salmon* Anglers however are generally provided with what is called a *gaff*, which is a stick something pliable, with a large *barbed* hook at the end, and which can be thrust into the head or gills of the fish, to lift him from the water; for which purpose a *landing net* is too small.)

The line from the *Reel*, after being run through the rings, is to be joined to the foot or gut length, which must be looped at each end, the one to fasten it to the *reel line*, the other to the *fly*; this *foot-length* must be made of *three* strong silk-worms guts twisted together, *three* lengths will be sufficient, as only *one* fly is used, the link to which the fly is fixed should be looped on the same way, for the convenience of changing it, if the fish refuse one sort of fly, and another is wished to be tried. It has been said, that the *colour* of the *fly* is of little consequence, provided it be *large*, and ribbed with *gold* or *silver* twist: . . .

Some variations of rod rings, showing the wide range of designs available during the 1880s. They were usually made of either brass or nickel.

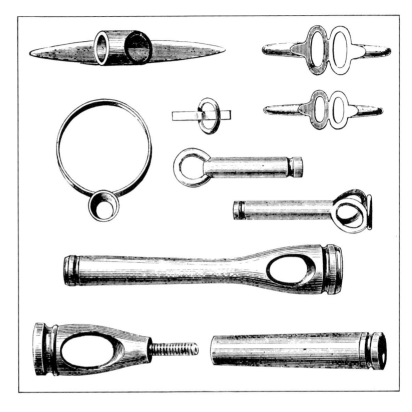

John Harrington Keene in his book *Fishing Tackle, Its Materials and Manufacture*, published in 1886, comments that the design of rods had remained virtually unaltered for the century prior to his book. He writes 'I have a fly rod in my posession at this moment which has probably killed tons of fish for it is over a century old; and yet its taper and general appearance is totally unimpaired, and the entire *toute ensemble* is quite comparable with some of the more costly finished weapons of this superlative age.' We might comment, yet another century on, that even now the changes that have taken place have hardly rendered early salmon rods unrecognizable.

For the majority of anglers the first half of the nineteenth century was a period of slow development. For obvious reasons of economy and availability, local woods were used in the construction of rods. Ash and yew were mainly used for butts, with the occasional use of chestnut and oak, while lancewood, red deal, hazel, withy and hornbeam met the requirements for flexibility for the upper sections. Ash and red deal were especially cheap and available and indeed ash was still popular in the 1880s. The type of ash used in rod making was known as ground ash, and was cut from young shoots of the common ash. It was strong, tough and elastic and not given to warping. It was also often used for the construction of billiard cues and one writer even suggested that a spent cue made an excellent butt for a fishing rod. Ash was of less use for the upper sections of the rod as it lacked strength if excessively tapered. However, it was very popular among early makers of salmon rods. Lancewood and red deal were invariably used for Nottingham-style rods.

By the 1880s local woods were being superseded by imported woods, mainly hickory, washaba, bethabara, greenheart, blue mahoe, snakewood and red locust. Hickory and greenheart were among the most popular foreign woods used by the commercial rod manufacturers.

Hickory, which was imported from America and Canada, was received in what were known as billets: V-shaped logs which were cut into planks on arrival. The tree grows to a height of 90 feet, and the timber is similar to walnut: strong, coarse-grained, elastic and tough, and of medium weight. It had to be well-seasoned and only the best quality was suitable for rod building. As the main disadvantage of hickory was that it tended to warp when coming into contact with water, its use was confined to the butt end, where its thickness prevented warping and its weight helped to balance the rod. Hickory was used for the cheaper fishing rods.

The Hardy patent bridge ring was fitted to most of their fly rods from 1891.

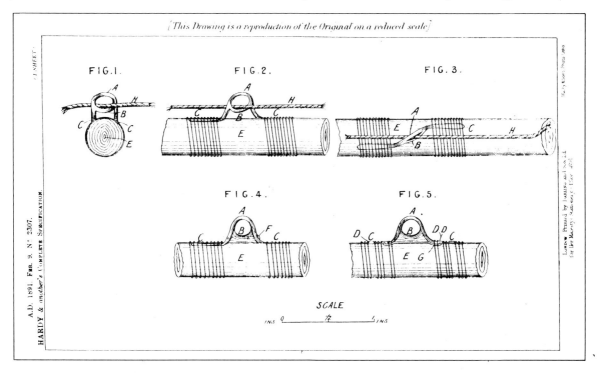

Greenheart, imported from British Guiana in the West Indies, was in extensive use in Britain in the construction of piers and breakwaters and for shipbuilding because of its capacity to withstand the erosion of salt water. Greenheart is taken from the Bibiri tree of the laurel family, which can grow up to 70 feet high. It varies in colour from a dark to a light, even yellowish, brown. Its chief disadvantage in rod building was its great weight, but this was amply compensated for in its flexibility and its capacity to take a very fine taper. Its tendency to warp while seasoning could be rectified by warming the wood gently and leaving it to season further under weights. Seasoning was an important process because if it was not completed properly the greenheart rod was liable to split like a carrot; this might also occur if the rod was allowed to dry out. Greenheart was immensely popular for rod making and continued to be used into the 1920s, long after the split-cane rods had gained their belated popularity in Britain.

Washaba, like greenheart, was imported from British Guiana and was akin to it in colour, strength and flexibility. However, it suffered from being even heavier and was difficult to work because it was very hard and permeated with a resin which blunted the edge of tools.

Blue mahoe was imported from Cuba and Jamaica and was of the mallow species, a tree which can grow to 50 feet. The wood is a dark greenish blue colour and, with a close grain, it takes a good polish. For the rod builder, blue mahoe had the advantage of being light, strong and resilient and so was especially efficient for trout rods. A 12-foot trout rod could be handled easily in difficult conditions and the wood's exceptional elasticity allowed the rod to hold its shape even if bent excessively. Such is its strengthened elasticity that in its native Cuba it was used for making springs for two-wheeled vehicles called *vollantes*.

Lancewood, imported from Guiana and Cuba, was also used in carriage building. The timber was light and elastic and was preferred by some makers for the tips of their fly rods to the heavier greenheart. It was easily worked and took a good polish.

Steelwood, or dagane, was a popular wood in America and was imported into Britain from its native Cuba from about 1885. It was, as its name suggests, very strong and flexible, and of a fibrous grain and yellow in colour, but heavy.

It is often difficult to identify the types of wood used in rod construction, not only due to the small amounts used, but also because of the frequent use of dark stains and varnishes.

This advertisement from the Fishing Gazette *gives the results of some of the extensive tests to which manufacturers, such as Hardys, subjected their equipment.*

TRUE VALUES of MATERIALS for ROD MAKING

The following *Extract* is from a report on tests carried out by W. H. Thorn, Esq., Memb. N.E.C.Inst. of Engineers, author of the "Engineers' Hand Book," etc., etc. The full report was given in Hardy's Catalogue for the year 1900 :—

DESCRIPTION OF TESTS

The first test to which the samples were submitted was that of deflection under a live load, that is to say, a weight of one pound was attached to each rod in such a manner as to be capable of falling a distance of 12 inches. At a distance of eighteen inches from the end a mark was made which corresponded with another on the holder. This was made of two pieces of hard wood with recesses to just take each rod, and then holder and rod securely clamped to a heavy and substantial frame top in such a manner as to allow the rod and attached weight to project from the top for 18 inches.

Another frame was erected sideways at the end of the rod, in such a way as to allow a drawing board of sufficient dimensions to move easily along on hard steel balls in order to reduce friction. At the extremity A of the rod a small pencil was inserted, and by moving the frame supporting the drawing board close up to the rod, the pencil was made to impinge on a sheet of paper securely stretched. The weight of 1 lb. was then raised to the level of the rod and secured by a catch ; when all was in readiness the detent was released, the weight fell for a distance of 12 inches, the drawing board moved along under influence of the weight, and the pencil at the extremity of the rod indicated in a graphic manner the vibrations of the specimen under test, and showed by the depth of the first vibration the resilience or proof load of the piece, and at the finish of its undulations recorded by a straight line the dead load deflection caused by **L lbs.** hanging at a distance of 18 inches.

This was done two or three times with each kind of rod, and the clearest curve chosen as the indication of that specimen. The example given is the curve obtained from rod No. 2. The line A B is the line drawn by the pencil when the rod was at rest, at B the falling weight took effect, and the end of the rod was

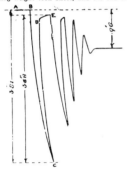

deflected for a distance of 3.81 inches, the recovery is shown by the curve C D, which in this case does not reach the zero line A B, the straighter portion D E is formed by the upward movement of the weight continuing after the end of the rod has almost recovered itself, and is shown rising to E. This indicates the endeavour of the rod to return to its original position ; but before it can do so the weight again falls, and so the wavy line is drawn, until the rod remains at rest under its dead load deflection.

The numerical analysis of all these curves is given in the tabulated statement herewith.

The next test was similar to the above, only substituting a 2 lb. weight in place of 1 lb., everything else being the same. At first sight it might be imagined that the deflection for 2 lb. would be twice that for 1 lb. ; but this is not so, the nature of the various woods prohibiting this.

The test following this was to stress the rods to breaking point. This was done by placing the rod in the same position and manner as before, attaching to the end of it a self-registering Salter balance ; through the hook of this passed a stout cord, leading to a block secured to an eyebolt in the ground, and on pulling the cord the rod gradually bent down until the stress became greater than the wood fibres could bear, and partition took place.

The final test was for specific gravity or relative weight. This was conducted in the usual manner, viz. : weighing in and out of distilled water, and revealed the fact that the skin of the bamboo was nearly 3½ times heavier than the fibres immediately inside.

BEHAVIOUR OF SPECIMENS WHILST UNDER TEST

Note.—All deflections caused by 1 lb. weight.

No. 1.—Deflection was here the least of any, both under live and dead loads ; the breaking weight was also very good indeed, fracture commencing at 12 lb. and going on until a maximum of 24 lb. was gained, at which point no further pressure could be registered, as any increase of stress only resulted in more bending. The specific gravity of this rod was larger, owing to it being double built, and having a steel centre. Its elasticity under live load was excellent, the rod recovering itself rapidly and completely, and in *no instance did any of this make go above the zero line*. Its rapidity of recovery was not so great as No. 2.

The total merit marks gained by No. 1 rod amounted to 39.4, being 4.8 ahead of the next best one. In testing some samples of this rod, the cement parted sooner than the wood fibres would give way, showing how great was the strength of the double built bamboo and steel combined.

The results given by this rod prove incontestibly that it is manufactured and designed on the best method, and, taking everything into consideration, shows that no other kind of rod can approach it.

The tabulated statement I have prepared for the double purpose of rendering comparisons of the rods more easy, and to avoid in this report a mass of bewildering repetitions, which would necessarily ensue if the merits and demerits of each separate rod were put into writing. In the statement the merit marks vary between 10 for the best and 0 for the worst ; so that a glance at any particular merit column will show the character of that rod for that particular trial. The column of total merit marks shows by proportionate division of 10 between the various rods, the final results of a series of experiments ; and the character of the various forms of rods may, I think, be judged from it with considerable accuracy. I may mention that the power of recovery has been calculated from the time of recovery which is proportional to the length of the curve described by the pencil when the rod was under live deflection. The rods have been tested as semi-beams, as it was thought that stress artificially applied in that manner was most in accordance with the natural stress induced in a rod when a fish was struck and played.

In the case of No. 1, the tempered steel centre gives greater elasticity to the arrangement without materially adding to the weight, a feature which must be of the utmost importance in casting against the wind, in which operation the whole life and energy of the rod must be thrown into the line.

When rods are steel centred there is an upward force inside the section, tending to move the rod back again to its original position ; so that two rods, having everything the same in both, but one steel centre and the other not, would show different deflections under the same load ; thus rods Nos. 1 and 2, when under test, showed that the steel centre gave perfect elasticity and a minimum amount of deflection under a given load, thus it will be seen that while steel rods are useless if not dangerous, a correct proportion of steel introduced into the rod is an improvement.

Number.	Section.	Kind of Rod.	Leverage.	Deflections 1 lb.			Deflection 2 lb.		Breaking weight.		Specific gravity.		Elasticity under lb.		Power of Recovery.		Total merit allowed.	REMARKS
				live.	dead.	merit marks.	live.	dead.	lbs.	merit marks.	S.G.	merit marks.	mrt. = 1	mrt. mks.	length of curve.	mrt. mks.		
1		Double-built cane, steel centre	18 in	3·8	0·72	10	7·08	2·28	12 to 24	10	1·147	0	1	10	22	9·4	39·4	Skin broke suddenly and fracture continued up to 24lb.
2		Double-built cane	18	3·81	0·96	9·02	7·96	2·84	11 to 22	8·07	1·088	1·64	0·97	5	21	10	33·73	Ditto, from 11 to 22 lb.

HARDY Bros. Ltd., ALNWICK   LONDON : 61, PALL MALL, S.W.1   EDINBURGH :   MANCHESTER : 12 to 14, Moult Street.   101, Princes Street.

While many woods were tried in the search for the perfect construction, there is no doubt that the most significant development of the century was in the use of bamboo cane. From slow beginnings the cane rod had developed into a triumph of craftsmanship and technology by the end of the century, gradually overtaking the conventional wood rods in popularity.

The bamboo canes used in rod making included the East Indian mottled, Spanish white, South Carolina and Japanese. Both the male and the female bamboos were used, the former being solid and the latter with hollow joints. One of the problems associated with importing such materials was the possibility of infestation with the larvae of wood-boring insects. To overcome this, the exporting countries would treat the canes by scorching, which frequently ruined them for the most fastidious rod makers. Canes were strong and elastic and the outer skin so hard that it was difficult to cut. The inner section was much softer and spongy so for a good split-cane rod this was cut away and substituted with another layer of the outer skin. Rods of this construction are known as 'double built'. Naturally a crucial element of such rods was the glue which held the finely tapered splints of cane together; the best-quality cement was known as 'Russian Isinglass'. Later in the history of cane rods, extra strength was added in the form of a steel core.

The development of the cane rod is associated with the American manufacturers in the second half of the nineteenth century. However, it is known that experiments were being made with cane in the early years of the century in Britain. Cane was then being imported into Britain in large quantities to supply the fashion for oriental style furniture made popular by the Prince Regent in his exotic Pavilion at

An early twentieth-century Hardy split-cane rod, owned by the author Ernest Hemmingway.

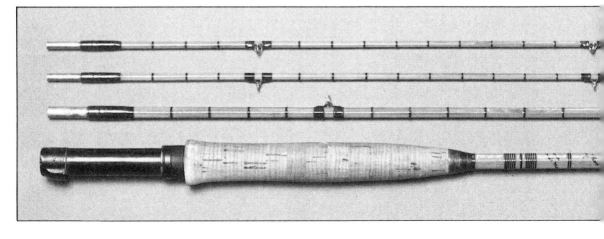

Brighton. Daniel, as early as 1807, mentions the use of bamboo cane in the construction of rods but does not refer to any precise method, nor to the splitting of the canes. It is possible that experiments were being carried out at this period on split canes as well as various woods, especially for the top sections, by binding together three sections of cane.

It would appear that the development was not an instant success and did not find favour in Britain until the 1870s. Three firms of tackle manufacturers, Ainge & Aldred, J.K. Farlow and J. Bernard, did however, include examples of the type on their stands at the Great Exhibition of 1851, and two years later Ainge & Aldred showed some examples on their stand at an exhibition in New York. A certain amount of cross-pollination of ideas no doubt occurred between rod makers on both sides of the Atlantic. It is recorded that a certain Mr James Alexander Stevens of Hoboken, New Jersey, visited the Great Exhibition in 1851 and that at that time he commissioned a split-cane rod from William Blacker of 54 Dean Street, London. He appears to have returned to the United States with this rod and took it the following year for repair to William Mitchell. It was of sufficient interest to the American rod restorer for him to have made a record of the rod.

While the early stages of one of the most important developments in the history of rod construction had taken place in Britain, it was in America that the idea came to fruition and became a commercial success. Prior to the 1840s rod building in the United States had been dominated by European influence, but there is evidence to suggest that, at that time, experiments in the use of split canes were being carried out simultaneously in various parts of America. This would have been quite likely, as the industry was still not organized and was dominated by a few large manufacturers.

An early proponent of the new craft and one of the first names to appear in split-cane rod building was Samuel Phillippe of Easton, Pensylvania, who constructed a rod for a well-known angler, Charles H. Luke. A writer for the *New York Times* in 1848, described the rod as being made of natural bamboo. Phillippe did not use cane exclusively, in common with most other early rod makers using the new material, who were perhaps unwilling to commit themselves completely to an untried method, and the butt section of early rods is mainly of wood, most often ash. The nodes of the cane were initially cut out and only the splines used, several of the short lengths being joined together to form a section.

Various other methods of employing cane were tried in the early years. In 1856 Bradford & Anthony, retailers of angling equipment, were importing split-cane rods from Aldred & Sons of London, some of some of which had the skin of the cane on the inside and some on the outside. It was some years before rod makers finally recognized the advantage of retaining the natural enamel of the cane on the exterior of the rod. Perhaps an explanation of the curious situation of an American retailer importing split-cane rods from Britain may lie in the fact that the market in America was booming for the new-style rods, while in Britain it was not. American makers could not keep pace with demand and British manufacturers no doubt were only too pleased to find an outlet for rods which were so painstaking to make.

At this early period, those sections of the rod that were constructed of bamboo were made of either three or four fillets of cane, according to the preference of the maker. It is known, however, that in about 1860, E.A. Green and Thaddeus Morris made for their own use, three-section rods, all sections of bamboo and all of four-strip cane. These appear to be the first rods built entirely of cane. Three years later, in 1863, Charles Murphy was the first to put this type of rod into commercial production. In 1865 Murphy made a salmon rod and, in the following year, a bass rod, both of the four-strip, split-cane type. Hard on the heels of these developments came the use, during the 1860s, of six strips of

One of the workshops at Allcock's Redditch factory. High quality rods of all types were produced in this factory.

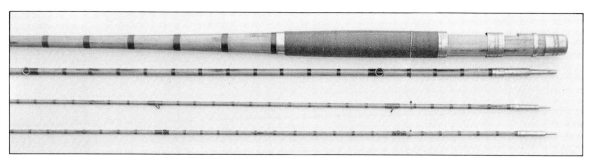

An American, Charles Murphy, is credited with being the inventor of the split-cane fly rod in about 1862. This early and rare example of his rods is in particularly good condition.

cane glued together. These thicker sections were appropriate for the butt and first sections, while the upper sections continued to be made of four strips.

It was Hiram Lewis Leonard, the doyen of the American rod manufacturers, who brought the long period of development of the split-cane rod to its peak. By 1870 he was constructing some of the finest split-cane rods in a fully developed form which was to be popular for many decades and can even be obtained to this day. Leonard was the first rod maker to use the strips of cane complete with the nodes, these being interspersed throughout the length of the rod to avoid any weak point. This, of course, necessitated having the skin exclusively on the outside. His rods, at first, were entirely of six-strip construction, but later he even introduced octagonal rods of eight strips and then twelve-strip, hexagonal, double-built, split-cane rods. By the mid-1870s he was reported to be making over two hundred rods per year. These were sold mainly by Andrew Clark & Co of New York, and Bradford & Anthony of Boston, until in 1877 Leonard went into partnership with William Mills & Son. Following this, in 1881, he moved his factory to Central Valley, New York, closer to the Mills family business in New York and closer to the main centres of demand.

Although Leonard was not the pioneer of the split-cane rod, he was certainly its most successful exponent. Keene, writing in 1886, described Leonard as 'the chief rod maker of the world'. A distinctive feature of Leonard's rods was the patent split-shoulder type of suction ferrule. The normal solid ferrule made of brass or nickel was found to be too unyielding for the especially elastic quality of cane. Another feature of the new ferrule was a small brass disc which was welded into the base of the ferrule to protect the exposed end of the cane from deterioration caused by mould formed by damp retained in the base of the ferrule. This patent ferrule was an important innovation which became widely copied. In 1893 Leonard produced the Catskill range of rods which were especially elegant, with cigar-shaped handles trimmed with a German silver (a nickel-silver alloy) butt cap and reel seat. The Fairy Catskill rod of 8 ft weighed only 2⅛ ounces, which was a extraordinary achievement for the period

In Britain, conventional wood rods continued in favour long after the new cane rods had been tried and tested in many waters. Some explanation for this may be found in Cholmondeley-Pennell's comment in his book, *Fishing (Salmon and Trout)*, published in 1893, where he explains that fly fishermen were put off split-cane rods because they doubted the cane rod's ability to take the strain imposed upon them. There was also a tendency for the glue to ooze out of the joints when wet, leaving the rod liable to come apart. He quotes Kelson's report of the Fisheries Exhibition, published in *The Field* on 27th October 1883. 'This is always the case sooner or later with these hand-made rods for salmon. But if eleven years' experience with them be admitted sufficient, I may say that the rods made with the machinery used by Messrs Hardy, who obtained the first prize for these split-cane rods at the Fisheries Exhibition, for cutting the cane perfectly true, obviate the difficulty satisfactorily.'

A writer in the *Fishing Gazette* in 1886 spoke disdainfully of cane rods: 'These little cane weapons are very artistic and tempting to the eye', but complained that they had no backbone. The editor of the *Gazette* went on to agree with the contributor. However, in a later edition, gave space for Hardy's to answer the complaint. Hardy's, who built both cane and wood rods took the attitude that they therefore had no axe to grind: 'All things new have a deal of prejudice to face, and all improvements have great difficulties to meet on this score.' They went on to state:

> Bamboo cane of the right class is admitted to be stiffer, lighter and tougher than any wood suitable for rod making. The law of forces teaches us that the formation of a hexagon by six equilateral triangles made from the same material, is stronger than one piece simply rounded. The layers of fibre in wood and cane run as the growth, and the layers of fibre in a built cane rod running parallel to the outside in each piece support each other, and although you may break the fibre in the piece which has its layer of fibre horizontal, it is supported by the triangle on either side, whose layers of fibre are at an angle of forty-five degrees to it. Then, again, in a round piece, whether cane or wood, you have a hard and soft side and as the layers of fibre are all parallel to each other, give no support.

A: a fine example of a late nineteenth-century American cane rod. It is 9½ ft long and the fittings are of nickel silver. The reel seat is stamped 'Dame Stoddard & Kendall, Boston, Neverbreak'. B: a three-piece splitwood salmon rod constructed of alternate strips of greenheart and lancewood. Towards the end of the last century it was owned by William Senior, Angling Editor of the Field *magazine who wrote under the pseudonym of* Red Spinner.

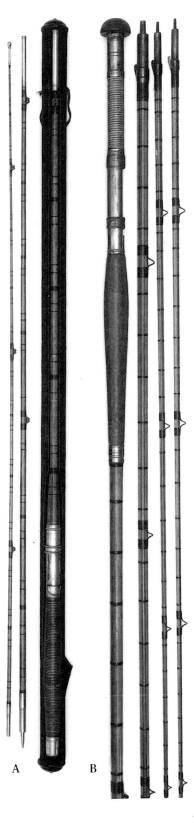

A   B

The writer went on to state that Hardy's had never had a cane-built joint broken, except in an accident, but many broken tops in greenheart rods. He also points out that in comparing cane with wood rods for stiffness in proportion to weight, the cane rods were substantially superior. A reviewer of a fisheries exhibition in 1896 also made the comment that Hardy's had recently discovered how to stain cane a good dark colour, which was a considerable improvement on the previous method of painting.

Although Hardy's were noted builders of wood rods, especially those made of greenheart, they were obviously prepared to back their judgement on cane rods even when noted writers and anglers were still implaccably opposed to them. They were proved to be right. Was this perhaps an early example of British invention receiving little encouragement at home but finding ready commercial response abroad? However, quantities of East India cane – Caroline white and jungle – were being imported into Britain in the final two decades of the century and were to endure in the industry longer than any of the solid woods. Split-cane rods can still be obtained in Britain and America, although the number of companies making them is now very small and the cost of these exquisite rods is very high.

As much as Hardy's might support the split-cane rod they were not about to put all their eggs in one basket. In the same article in the *Fishing Gazette* the company stated that they had been experimenting with over two hundred types of wood, many of which had never been imported into Britain before. Out of this prodigious number they finally selected three and had imported several tons of each for making up into rods. For reasons of commercial wisdom, the three were not to be named until production was in an advanced state. They were prepared to disclose, however, that of the new woods, greenheart was still most suitable for top sections.

The bad publicity received by cane rods was in no small measure due to inferior examples coming on to the market at prices which the average angler could afford. Quantities of cane, rejected by the major manufacturers as substandard, or damaged by the scorching process, were sold to the mass producers. Another problem facing the quality manufacturers was that of pirating. Hardy's, in their catalogue of 1888, warn anglers to beware of mass-produced American split-cane rods, imported into Britain and passed off as having been made there. William Mills & Son of New York suffered similar problems as late as the 1920s. In response to cheap European and American copies being passed off as genuine Leonard rods, the company began to stamp the reel seat or butt cap of their rods to denote the real thing.

The rods made by the craftsmen of the leading companies were obviously of a high quality and were cherished by the anglers of the day as they are now by collectors. This is not to say that the mass-produced rods were all inferior copies. The major tackle manufacturers of America — Heddon, Shakespeare, Southbend, Granger, Edward vom Hofe and Orvis — all made large quantities of split-cane rods and high-quality rods in this category are very desirable to the collector.

However, the collector of fishing rods faces some difficulties. It is not unusual for rods, especially split-cane rods, to have undergone total refurbishment in their lifetime. Some manufacturers stamped their name on the reel fittings or the but cap, but others inscribed the name and other particulars in Indian ink just above the handle. In the process of rewhipping and revarnishing the rod, such marks have often been removed. While a correct attribution can usually be made of a craftsman-made rod from, say, Leonard or Hardy, even without the name, it can be far from easy in the case of the more anonymous factory rod. Another hazard for the collector is the rod with replaced sections. It was not unusual for a hard-working rod to have a damaged section replaced, and not necessarily by the original manufacturer. So it can often be the case that an indentifying feature of a rod is missing, making it extremely difficult to make a satisfactory attribution. As with antique furniture, if a repair has been carried out fifty or even a hundred years ago the process of ageing makes it difficult to detect.

Naturally, the main interest for the collector is in classic rods by the major manufacturers. There were, and continue to be, many companies making rods of all types but it is rarity and quality which determine the value of the item. A named specimen will be of greater interest than a similar piece with no mark on it.

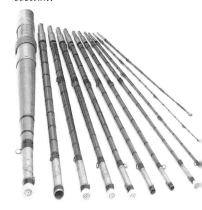

A rare three-strip split-cane, valise rod, probably mid nineteenth century. It is a ten-piece, 11 ft rod with drop rings, nickel silver spiggot ferrules, and black-lined, turned ivory buttons on each section.

III *A nineteenth-century trout rod with brass crank-handled reel by Farlows, a painted wooden creel and an ash-framed landing net with brass fittings.*

IV *The legendary Allcock's Ariel reel.*

CHAPTER TWO

British reels

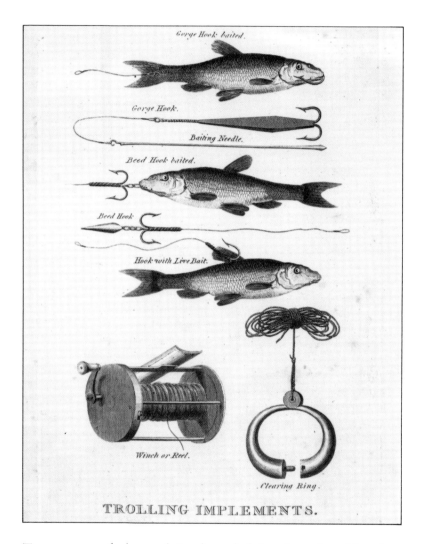

Gorge Hook baited.

Gorge Hook.

Baiting Needle.

Beed Hook baited.

Beed Hook.

Hook with Live Bait.

Winch or Reel.

Clearing Ring.

TROLLING IMPLEMENTS.

An early nineteenth-century engraving depicting methods of mounting live bait, with an illustration of a contemporary multiplying reel and brass clearing ring.

THE ORIGIN of the reel is shrouded in obscurity. The first mention of it in British angling literature appears in Barker's *Art of Angling*, published in London in 1651. Izaac Walton makes no mention of the reel in the first edition of *The Compleat Angler* of 1653, but when he does make reference to it in the second edition two years later, he dismisses it as something others use. No individual is credited with the invention of such a significant item of the angler's equipment.

For at least two centuries reels were invariable referred to as 'wynches' and the term continued to be used well into this century, alongside the term 'reel', with apparently no distinction between the two. The Allcock catalogue, as late as 1937/8, refers to their Felton Cross Winch.

The fact that no European is credited with the invention of the reel is perhaps because no European did invent it. A writer in the *Japan Mail* in 1885, reviewing an exhibition of Chinese antiquities then recently opened in Tokyo, describes a painting by an artist of the Sung Dynasty (960 to 1280) depicting fishermen with reels attached to their rods. It therefore appears that fishing reels are yet another invention, relatively modern to the West, which had long existed in China. Perhaps it is not beyond the bounds of possibility that an eleventh-century reel will be discovered in the tomb of a keen angler emperor, or at least a mandarin, who was intent on making sure he continued to enjoy his beloved sport beyond the grave.

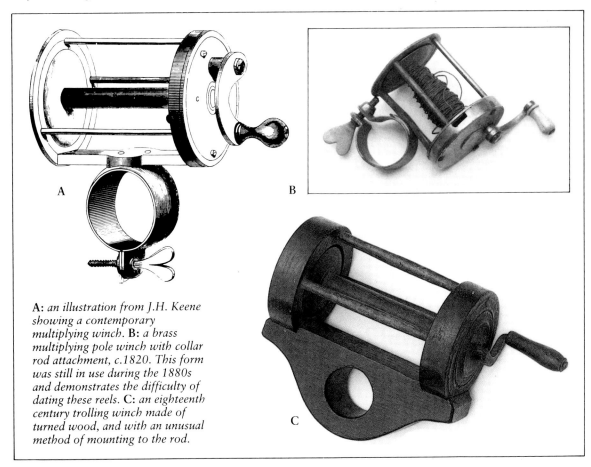

A: *an illustration from J.H. Keene showing a contemporary multiplying winch.* B: *a brass multiplying pole winch with collar rod attachment, c.1820. This form was still in use during the 1880s and demonstrates the difficulty of dating these reels.* C: *an eighteenth century trolling winch made of turned wood, and with an unusual method of mounting to the rod.*

A & C: *two examples of early nineteenth-century pole winches, neither of which is named. The side view clearly shows the offset crank handle of the multiplying form.* **B:** *a brass fly reel by Bowness & Bowness; a well established London tackle company, which started business in the late seventeenth-century. We are able to date this reel as after 1876, because of the registered design mark which appears on the crank handle.* **D:** *another London tackle maker, Eaton & Deller, produced this 4¾ in. half wood and brass salmon reel, in the late 1800s.* **E:** *a rare example of a large Scottish pirn, from the eighteenth century. The end plates are walnut, connected by four oak pillars.*

However ancient the ancestry of the reel may be, as far as the West is concerned its rapid technological development in this century perhaps obscures the fact that up to 150 years ago many anglers enjoyed their sport without the aid of a reel of any kind, fishing in the roach pole manner. Modern anglers have available to them an enormous range of highly sophisticated machines to cater for every condition anywhere in the world and to suit every nuance of taste for the sport. For at least 200 years anglers who were sufficiently keen, or who could afford such a luxury, used the simplest form of reel to perform the simplest task required of a reel — that of storing a line, letting it out and returning it when required.

Early winches were of a simple, closed-end construction, which formed the basis of all subsequent developments; the Scottish rolling winch, known as a Pirn, is a rare early example of this type. The end plates were of turned wood, usually of walnut, cherry or oak but sometimes of one of the newly imported hardwoods, such as mahogany or, occasion-

ally, rosewood, both of which were being imported in quantity in the eighteenth century for the furniture trade. The end plates were linked by wood or iron pillars, forming a cylindrical cage. On the basic centre-pin reel the drum revolved on a brass spindle and was retained by a small latch or thumb screw; a ratchet attached to the side plate checked the revolutions of the drum. The rod fitting consisted of a simple saddle or wood clamp.

Pirns are amongst the earliest form of reel and are the earliest datable examples to come on the market. As such they appear to be earlier than the centre-pin reel which, having an 'open-ended' axle, required more sophisticated construction techniques. Few of the early winches have survived, but the form continued into the nineteenth century with little change. The scarce early models are difficult to date accurately, but later examples are available.

Even after the advent of the winch many anglers continued to fish in the traditional manner, with the line being simply tied to the tip. Some coarse fishermen have, of course, continued to favour this method, especially during match fishing tournaments and in France, where the pole is still favoured by many for catching different species of fish. Instead of winding in the line with a reel they quickly disjoint the roach pole. To compensate for lack of reach and flexibility, rods became longer, until by the middle of the nineteenth century they were commonly 15 to 24 feet long.

The long rods for coarse and fly fishing to some extent avoided the need for a reel, as they could reach over most rivers. However, with the desire to increase the range of the sport, the potential of the reel began to be recognized. A longer line, not only stored but also controlled by the reel, brought to the angler greater ability to play the fish. Contrary to popular belief, the multiplier is not of twentieth-century origin; it was developed in the late eighteenth century but its use was limited to line storage. It was a simple form of geared reel with the addition of a crank handle, referred to by contemporary writers as a 'multiplying winch'. The first examples were constructed of wood, but later more usually of brass, and it is probable that the finest examples were made by clock- and watchmakers.

As is common with new developments they were not universally popular. Even a century later the well-known angling writer, Francis Francis, commented that in his opinion the best thing an angler could do with a multiplyer was to give it away. However the *Fishing Gazette* took a more enlightened view. Reviewing a reel sent to them by

The first model Nottingham winch, made of mahogany with ivory handles; the collar rod fitting is of brass. It is unusual to find Nottinghams with the collar attachment.

A nineteenth-century brass salmon reel with raised pillars, the winding arm turning within the anti-foul rim. The fixed check on this example is located in a raised housing on the back plate.

Smith & Wall, wholesale manufacturers of fishing reels located in Birmingham, the writer referred to it enthusiastically as a very ingenious novelty.

> The grand advantage of a multiplier is that it enables you to wind in quickly; one turn of the handle of this reel sends the spool round nearly three times.
>
> But the novelty in this nicely-made winch is that by pressing a trigger you can disconnect the spool. The object of this arrangement is to permit of a light bait being cast from the reel. To prevent overrunning, there is a brass stud on the back of the winch, which is lightly pressed as the cast is made. Directly the bait touches the water you press the trigger, and can then wind in with the multiplier. It will require a little practice to master this winch, but we think it quite probable that it will become a favourite with many anglers. The Americans would appreciate it for bait casting.

Once improvements began the movement gathered momentum. The well-known writer on angling, H. Cholmondeley-Pennell, indicated the great changes that had taken place by 1883, when the Great Fisheries Exhibition displayed to the angling world the new horizons the industrial revolution was opening up for a traditional sport. He wrote:

> The Fisheries Exhibition of 1883 was prolific in new reels, many of which, it must be confessed, were not only highly ingenious as inventions but really excellent in their adaptation to different sorts of fishing. Indeed, if reels have not in the matter of 'improvement' quite kept pace with the improvements in rods, they are yet prodigiously in advance of the unmechanical windlasses with which our forbears, in the not very distant past, were content to reel in the victims of their prowess. But I will not slay the slain twice over, or evoke, merely for the purpose of exorcising them, the ghosts of 'Pirns,' 'winch-winders,' 'multipliers' (*horresco referens!*) and other similar abominations, which if not actually as extinct as the dodo, soon will be . . .

Clearly the union of sport and technology had already taken place, spawning a plethora of patents. Some of these were to form the basis of important developments, but many were not to survive beyond a single idea. This quest for the ideal equipment to aid the sportsman, to increase his pleasure and improve his performance, continues unabaited to this day.

Much of this development has stemmed from the basic centre-pin reel. A prime nineteenth-century example is the

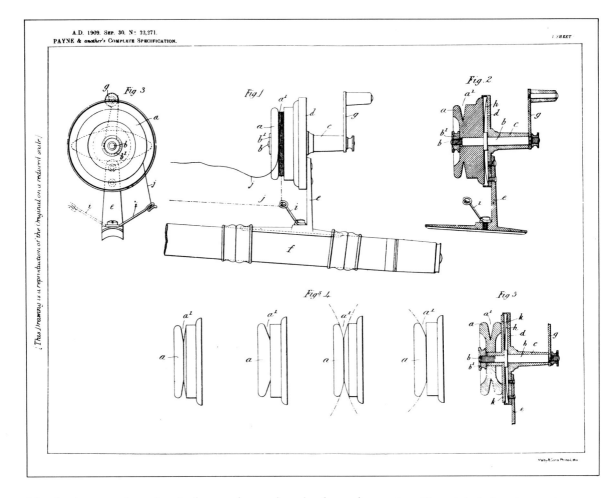

A.D. 1909. Sep. 30. N° 22,271.
PAYNE & another's Complete Specification.

I SHEET

Nottingham reel, a simple form of wood reel adapted to suit the particular conditions and style of fishing in the Midlands. Many modifications in its evolution can be seen throughout the nineteenth century, and it continued to be made in quantities well into this century. The addition of brass mounts to the back plate in the form of a star were made to correct the wood reel's main disadvantage, that of swelling and warping when wet. Various alloys, or even silver, were also applied for the same purpose. The style of early reels was fairly standard for all types of angling in river or sea, the variations being mainly in size to accommodate more or less line.

Few of the early reels can be attributed to a particular maker for few are named, but towards the end of the nineteenth century the practice of stamping the name or trade mark of the manufacturer became common. Where the name of the retailer appears on a reel there is little indication of the

The original elevations and cross-sectional drawings submitted with the Payne and Chippendale patent application.

42

A: *a nineteenth-century brass crank-handled pole winch with a leather lined collar and wing nut for attachment to the rod. This method of securing the winch to the rod lasted until the end of the century.* **B:** *a brass pole winch from the early 1800s, showing an alternative method of fixing which used a spiked foot and wing nut.* **C:** *a very rare example of Frederick Skinner's Archemedian reel, registered in Sheffield 25 April 1848.* **D:** *a late eighteenth-century trolling winch made of iron and brass.* **E:** *a brass crank-handled reel by J. Jones which was fitted with a folding ivory knob to avoid damage in transit. The design registration date, 20 March 1843, is inscribed* *on the winding arm. At this time Jones was working at Princes Street, Leicester Square, London.* **F:** *a Chippendale patent casting reel, No. 23, made by J.E. Miller.* **G;** *a bronzed brass multiplying reel by J.E. Miller, 'The Reffitt Moore Rapid.* **H;** *a Slater patent ebonite reel, showing the famous Slater latch which holds the drum on the spindle.* **I:** *the well-known 4½ in. Coxon Aerial reel.* **J:** *a raised pillar salmon reel by H.L. Leonard.*

actual maker, since the manufacture of reels at this period was still in the nature of a cottage industry. The designer and patent holder may well not have been an established manufacturer and he would have put the work out to many craftsmen working anonymously. Standard patterns were also mass produced in Birmingham and distributed to retailers; if these are marked at all, it is with the retailer's name only. British reels from as early as the seventeenth century are occasionally found inscribed only with a date. This is most likely to record a presentation, especially as some also bear names which are probably those of the recipients.

Among the leading manufacturers of fishing equipment in the second half of the nineteenth century was Slater of Newark-on-Trent. He first established his factory in about 1850, at first catering to the local 'bottom' anglers, who had perfected a technique for catching species of fish, for example carp, which mainly fed off lake or river beds. His business gradually expanded to include all aspects of angling, catering to a large national market and producing many variants of the Nottingham reel. His most famous reel is known as Slater's Combination Reel, so called because it incorporated a pillar system on a mahogany centre-pin reel. While still made of wood and brass, the use of brass was extended to include a brass plate, instead of wood supported on brass pillars. This reduced excess play and friction, common to the wood reel. The reviewer of the Fisheries Exhibition, held in the Royal Westminster Aquarium, wrote warmly of the invention in the *Angler's Gazette* in 1896:

> It is a good many years since we first saw Mr Slater's first modification of the "Nottingham" reel without bars and the ordinary reel with bars and named it for him "Slater's Combination and Ordinary Reel", and since then it has been known as "Slater's Combination Reel". At this exhibition he shows an improvement upon it made of mahogany, 4 in. in diameter, at 17s. 6d. It is a grand reel. He also shows the same reel with a diameter of 7 in., for sea fishing. It certainly seems to us that it would answer admirably for tarpon fishing. The narrow barrel and great diameter will take in line as fast as any multiplier. It would want a good check for tarpon; in fact, we are sorry Mr Slater has omitted the check in the samples he shows.

For the benefit of anglers unfamiliar with tarpon, it is a powerful sea fish found mainly off the east coast of America, in the Florida Keys area; it is also found off certain North African coasts. Weighing up to 200 pounds and more, it is a great fighting fish and is often taken by anglers on light class tackle using either bait or fly, the latter being now preferred.

Slater's Combination Reel was in fact made with a check or ratchet. Having a free running action it cast well and was excellent for both trolling and for fly fishing. Another wood reel which Slater produced at the end of the century was the Scarborough pattern, used commonly on the coast of Yorkshire for casting from the beach. Not unlike a Nottingham reel, but of simpler comstruction, it was unusual in that the line was wound round in the reverse of the normal method. The line, when wound in with the right hand, came in a straight line from the rod to the top of the reel. This reduced the friction with the butt ring during casting, enabling the angler to achieve greater distances, but the method required considerable skill and judgement.

Other reels produced by Slater towards the end of the nineteenth century are made of brass, ebonite and aluminium and are all marked 'Slater's Patent'. The drum-catch, which is a distinctive feature of the Slater's Combination Reel, although patented, was widely copied and often appears on reels by various other makers.

Many of the early manufacturers were themselves keen anglers. Who better to recognize the limitations of their equipment and to know the improvements likely to find a ready market among the rapidly growing number of anglers?

P.D. Malloch of Perth, a casting champion and a skilled angler, designed and marketed a number of interesting reels. Malloch's Casting Reel, sometimes knows as Malloch's Spinning Reel, patented in 1884, was the first to rotate 90 degrees to allow the line to uncoil from the face of the drum. A contemporary writer in the *Scottish Field* commented that spinning had undoubtedly become popular on account of the Malloch reel and that it had 'reduced spinning to a sort of mechanical operation'. The truism 'time will tell' certainly applied to this important reel, for it remained in production for about 50 years, throughout a period of great innovation in reel design. The company also made two improvements to its No. 1 model: the addition of an optical check mechanism and a quick release for the drum. It did not withdraw the original model, but sold both versions concurrently.

The No.1 model was originally made of brass with a dull bronze finish but was later offered in either gunmetal or aluminium. Sizes varied from $2\frac{5}{8}$ inch, which in gunmetal weighed 10 ounces, to $4\frac{1}{2}$ inch, which weighed 32 ounces. In aluminium the same sizes were offered: $2\frac{5}{8}$ inch, weighing $6\frac{1}{2}$ ounces and the $4\frac{1}{2}$ inch, weighing 21 ounces.

A Malloch patent 'Brake' salmon fly reel, stamped with the famous oval trademark.

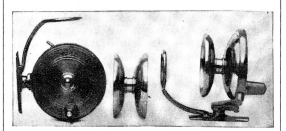

Malloch's Patent Spinning Reel

"Its friends have made it famous."

No. 1 Model
Reversible Drum and Optional Check

In Gun Metal.				In Aluminium.		
No.		Approx. Weights.	No.			Approx. Weights.
142	2⅝ inches	10 oz.	40/-	146	2⅝ inches	6½ oz.	45/-
143	3¼ inches	21 oz.	47/6	147	3¼ inches	14 oz.	52/6
144	4 inches	27 oz.	55/-	148	4 inches	18 oz.	60/-
145	4½ inches	32 oz.	60/-	149	4½ inches	21 oz.	67/6

Guide to Sizes

2⅝ inches	...	for Trout.	4 inches	...	for Salmon.
3¼ inches	...	for Small Salmon.	4½ inches	...	for Mahseer.

The 4-inch size carries 120 yards No. 3 Level "Kingfisher" Line.

Instructions

The cast is made by swinging the rod round behind the angler. It is then brought smartly forward until the rod completes a semi-circle and is in line with the objective. The line, which up to this point has been pressed against the rod butt by the forefinger, is released, and runs over the side of the drum. See page 29, figure A.

After the cast is made the reel is again turned to the first position, and the line wound up slowly and evenly on to the drum. Figure B.

In making the cast the drum is turned horizontally, and the line wound up until the gut trace is within a foot of the top ring of rod.

Easiest Spinning Reel in existence to master.

Malloch's Patent Spinning Reel

No. 2 Model
with "Gibbs" Patent Locking Lever

	Gun Metal.				Aluminium.		
No.	Size	Weight.	Price.	No.	Size	Weight.	Price.
150	3¼ ins.	21 oz.	55/-	153	3¼ ins.	14 oz.	60/-
151	4 ins.	27 oz.	60/-	154	4 ins.	18 oz.	65/-
152	4½ ins.	32 oz.	65/-	155	4½ ins.	21 oz.	70/-

Prices include Reversible Drum and Optional Check.

Special Features

(a) Locking Lever is so arranged that it unlocks reel, and further movement sets drum into casting position.

(b) Reversing above movement brings drum into winding-in position, and securely locks the reel.

(c) Both operations are performed without lifting hands from rod : herein lies the difference—a most important one—and a great improvement on our Standard Model.

(d) "Reversible Drum" { By simply pressing a spring, drum can be removed and reversed in a second.

(e) "Optional Check" { Saves check from undue wear and gives greater ease when winding in line.

Important :—To entirely obviate kinking attach a double swivel to the main line as shewn in illustration. Anglers will find this simple and efficient.

The writer in the *Scottish Field* favoured 'this most simple of all spinning reels' above all others. He did, however, refer to a common criticism, that of a tendency of kinking the line, but dismissed this as carried too far and the fault easily corrected by taking care to wind the line evenly on the drum. 'Most useful in difficulties', was how Secombe Grey described the Malloch reel in *Pike Fishing*: 'You can fish where others can't.' A certain Captain W.A. Knott of Norfolk was quoted in the 1936 catalogue as favouring the Malloch reel for sea fishing because with it casting from the shore with heavy weights was made easy.

The No. 2 model reel, apart from the Gibbs Patent Locking Lever, was otherwise identical to the No. 1 model. Malloch's 1938 catalogue set out the advantages of this reel:

(a) the locking lever is so arranged that it unlocks reel and further movement sets drum into casting positions:

Details taken from a Malloch catalogue of the late 1930s, showing the wide range of options available on their sidecaster spinning reels.

(b) reversing above movement brings drum into winding-in position, and securely locks reel;

(c) both operations are performed without lifting hands from rod — herein lies the difference, a most important one and a great improvement on our standard model;

(d) reversible drum — by simply pressing spring, drum can be removed and reversed in a second;

(e) optional check — saves check from undue wear and gives greater ease when winding in.

IMPORTANT NOTE: to entirely obviate kinking attach a double swivel to main line.

The No. 3 model, known as the Malloch-Erskine Patent Spinning Reel, developed as a result of the suggestion of a certain Colonel J. Erskine that the need to wind in the line in an anticlockwise direction, after reversing the drum, was 'somewhat troublesome, and liable in the excitement of the moment, to lose a fish'. His ingenious solution was to introduce into the reel, which again to outward appearance remained unaltered, a set of geared cog wheels and certain modifications to the drum which, when reversed, enabled the angler to continue to wind in the line using a clockwise turn of the handle. The No. 3 model was also made in hardened aluminium and was available in three sizes:

$2\frac{7}{8}$ inch weighing 13 ounces and costing 65 shillings
$3\frac{1}{4}$ inch weighing 17 ounces and costing 75 shillings
4 inch weighing 21 ounces and costing 80 shillings

It was also available with optional check, patent reversible drum, multiplying gear and Gibbs locking lever. It is curious that the No. 1 model should have continued to be in demand when, for the additional cost of only five or six shillings, a greatly improved version was available for many years.

Another of Malloch's inventions was the Sun and Planet Reel, so named from the relationship of a large cog to a smaller which controlled the amount of drag applied during the playing of a fish, through pressure on the handle. Thus the angler never needed to remove his hand from the handle when in action. An especially important feature, for which the reel was unique, was that the revolving plate and handle remained stationary while a fish was taking out line. The handle could not, therefore, become entangled with any obstacle while in use. This feature made it especially suited to trolling from a boat, where the line is dragged along by the forward motion of the boat, a good oarsman being a necessary part of the equipment. The reel rested on the

A Malloch's patent Sun and Planet Reel.

bottom of the boat and, as the winding plate did not revolve, there was no danger of the line catching on any object and thereby allowing the fish to break loose.

Recommended as a premier salmon fly reel, it was originally constructed in brass but, by 1930, was made of ebonite, bound with nickel silver. It was also available in specially hardened aluminium alloy. The ebonite version was available in six sizes, from 3¾ inches to 5 inches, and the aluminium version in seven, from 3½ inches to 5 inches. Prices ranged from 40 shillings to 65 shillings.

One satisfied customer, Douglas W. Clinch of New York, was reported in the Malloch catalogue of 1935 to have found that the Sun and Planet Reel was the only one he had observed not to go wrong in any conditions when used on Canadian salmon rivers. This appears to be borne out by the fact that a recent Canadian reel, the Valentine, made in the 1970s, works on exactly the same principle.

Malloch's reels are all marked. They are stamped with either 'P D Malloch, Perth' arranged in an oval, or simply 'Malloch, Patent', also in an oval.

R. Heaton was another leading manufacturer, with premises at 161-165 Upper Hospital Street, Birmingham, who is believed to have produced reels in substantial quantities and sold them on a wholesale basis to a number of retailers. One of the inventions which has earned Heaton a place in angling posterity was his Strike from the Winch Reel. This enabled the angler to set the hook on striking a fish, the drum tightening with a sudden pull on the line. Heaton's reels, which are predominantly of brass, are all stamped with his name on the winding plate.

H. Cholmondeley-Pennell, as well as being an angling writer and keen participant in the sport, had held the position of Her Majesty's Inspector of Sea Fisheries. He set about the task of inventing the ideal sea and salmon fishing reel and combined all the best features in existing reels to produce a refined from of crank-handled reel which would meet his specific requirements. Pennell's Reel extended the use of the crank handle to give more control and winding power. In his book *Fishing*, from the Badminton Library series published in 1893, Cholmondeley-Pennell describes his design process in considerable detail.

It is interesting to note that in 1893 a lightweight reel was of prime concern. Pennell considered using aluminium but discounted this on the grounds of its exorbitant cost at that time; it was not long, however, before the advantages began to outweigh the cost and aluminium was widely used for

A: a good example of a named brass pole winch by Ustonson, who was a London tackle maker during the late eighteenth century. B: a nineteenth-century pole winch. The pierced saddle of this reel was designed to take a leather pad, which acted as a cushion, between it and the rod. C: an early nineteenth-century crank-handled salmon reel. The interesting features of this reel are the raised case containing the fixed check, and the folding ivory knob on the crank handle. D: a fine example of a late Victorian crank-handled salmon reel made by Eaton & Deller of 6/7 Crooked Lane, London. E: a nineteenth-century bronzed brass trolling winch by Farlows of London. It was fitted with an anti-foul crank handle (by placing the handle under a slight rim, close to the face plate which prevents the line becoming trapped behind the handle). B & C are still loaded with the original horsehair line.

A Malloch's patent sidecaster spinning reel.

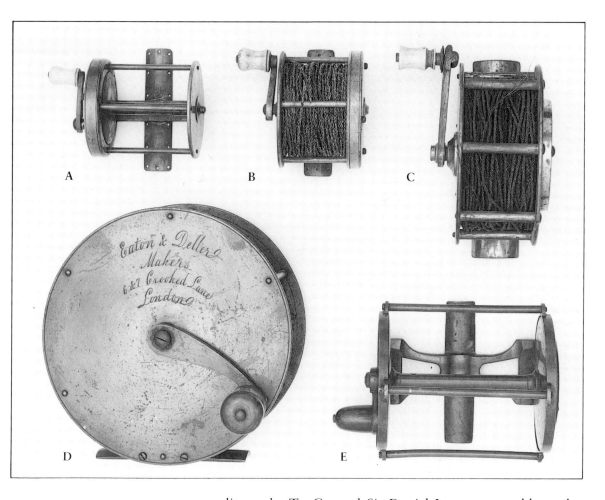

A   B   C

D   E

quality reels. To General Sir Daniel Lyson, a notable angler of the time, Pennell attributes the idea of combining the side and anti-foul rim in one solid piece of metal with the result that the handle terminates inside the rim, which both guards the handle and prevents the line tangling in it. It also obviates the need for an exterior side plate, thus reducing weight and adding strength and leverage. The check mechanism, covered with a hinged lid, tight enough to be almost watertight and opened by the point of a knife, is accessible for servicing and in an emergency, without taking the reel apart. The Pennell reel is 4½ inches in diameter, to take up to 150 yards of line, the amount needed for salmon fishing.

It would appear that Pennell did not patent his design, perhaps because it was a combination of other people's ideas. Numerous manufacturers produced variants of the Pennell Reel, the one by Farlow's of London being the closest to Pennell's own design.

Pennell's concern was about the high cost of aluminium soon to be left behind. At the Fisheries Exhibition of 1896, the reviewer from *The Fishing Gazette* noted an aluminium trout reel on the stand of Carter & Company, priced at 12s 6d and remarked on how reasonable the price seemed when, only a few years before, it would have been three or four times as much. Carter & Company also offered a reel made of another new material, xylonite, an early form of plastic which, it was claimed, was stronger than ebonite. A sea fishing reel by Carter & Company had gunmetal bearings and check action to avoid rusting; it was 6 inches in diameter and, in 1896, retailed for 12s 6d.

Cholmondeley-Pennell also turned his skills to adapting the famous Orvis Trout Reel, developed in America by Charles F. Orvis and imported into Britain. As this was the first fully perforated reel it marks an important stage in reel design. The purpose of the perforations was to allow the silk line to some extent to dry on the reel, but the reduction in weight was also of great benefit. Pennell also adapted the original Orvis handle; the result is known as the Orvis Pennell Reel.

The Fisheries Exhibition of 1883 may have been the showcase for British developments, but many new ideas were coming from America and having their effect on British reel design. The wood reels, with their disadvantages of warping and jamming when wet, were being replaced with reels made of a mixture of alloys, vulcanite, aluminium and ebonite. Brass reels, handsome and appealing as they are to collectors, were heavy, and skeleton reels, such as the Billinghurst and Follet from America, were soon to render them obsolete. The reduction in weight was an important factor in the new reels' success, together with the increased ventilation they gave to the line, which at this period had to be dried and reconditioned each time it was used.

A: *a Hardy 'Hercules' bronzed brass revolving plate fly reel.* **B:** *a good example of a presentation fly reel. It is engraved with the recipient's name and date of the presentation.* **C:** *a brass crank-handled reel by J.D. Dougal, Glasgow.* **D:** *a 2¾in. wide drum Perfect fly reel by Hardy's of Alnwick.*

A   B   C   D

The external and internal views of a Pennell reel.

The rapid development in technology and the booming market produced keen rivalry on both sides of the Atlantic. New inventions were patented in great quantities in America and Britain and promoted through the publication of company catalogues and the developing international mail-order business, and companies in both countries complained of copying and infringement of patents. The forerunners of the spinning reel began to appear in Britain at the turn of the century, with a number of companies and individuals patenting their variations. The P. D. Malloch Side Casting Reel, patented in 1884 and already discussed, was a reel of this type; its modernised version, the Malloch Erskine Patent reel, was still available in the 1930s.

A. H. Illingworth's famous Thread Line Spinning Reel was another variation which was patented in 1905. This reel too developed over a long production period lasting into the 1930s, with variants No. 1, No. 2, No. 3 and No. 4. The entry describing Illingworth's reel in the catalogue of W. J. Cummins, rod makers and retailers of Bishop Auckland, undated but published about 1930, explains the function of the reel and the advantage it claimed over its competitors:

The No. 3 model of the Illingworth reel is identical in principle with the previous two reels which it supersedes, but it has been greatly improved in several details.

The Principle – The problem solved by the late Mr

Alfred Holden Illingworth was how to throw a light and tethered bait, such a lightly leaded minnow, unprecedented distances. The line is drawn from the stationary spool of all models of the Illingworth reels just as readily as the slightest weight will draw cotton sideways from a full reel. When the weight ceases to act, the line ceases to come off the spool and overrunning is, therefore, unknown. To use heavy lines in conjunction with the light baits is as futile as to expect a projected feather to drag a rope through the course of its flight. The Illingworth reel, with its light line permits a light bait to be cast far and accurately because the line is light. It is barely thicker than cotton and weighs so little that it exerts an almost negligible drag upon the lightly leaded flight and minnow used for trout spinning and the bait is therefore free to travel the maximum distance that it can be thrown by the aid of a rod.

Why a Fish does not break the thin Line – To use such thin lines with any other system of reel is to court certain disaster; in the Illingworth reel a mechanical arrangement of give and take prevents disaster when playing a heavy fish and at the same time keeps a tight line upon it. If the fish is exerting a greater strain than the line will withstand, the reel yields line. If, on the other hand, the line is stronger than the pull exerted by the fish, the angler takes in line. In short, the reel provides for everything, including a motionless equipoise with equal weight of power balancing each other.

An Illingworth No. 1 threadline casting reel in its original velvet lined, kidney shaped, leather case: still retaining its oil bottle and folding screwdriver.

A New Feature to prevent the Line from Piling – The principle by which the line is recovered by the Illingworth reel corrects the twist put into it on being drawn off the spool and, when winding in, the spool rises and falls and seems to breathe to prevent the line from piling irregularly and on one part binding the other, which would interfere with the frictionless delivery of the line.

A Deep Drum ensures Line Economy – In the interest of line economy the front part of the spool is capable of being screwed away from its back portion to admit the insertion of the line backing which takes the form of cork discs with a central hole, which is supplied with the reel in various sizes. The advantage here is that on the line becoming worn, the frayed portion is cut off and cast away and a larger cork backing inserted to raise the line again almost to the level of the spool's lip, a position it should occupy in order that the bait may withdraw it easily and without friction. This process can be repeated until practically the whole of the line is exhausted.

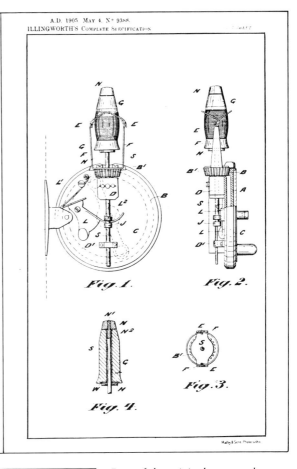

N.º 9388   A.D. 1905

Date of Application, 4th May, 1905
Complete Specification Left, 3rd Nov., 1905—Accepted, 4th Jan., 1906

PROVISIONAL SPECIFICATION.

Improvements in and relating to "Bait Casting Reels" used in Angling.

I, ALFRED HOLDEN ILLINGWORTH, of 2, Highclere Villas, Ben Rhydding, in the County of York, Wool Merchant, do hereby declare the nature of this invention to be as follows:—

This invention relates to improvements in what are known as "bait casting reels," used in angling, and has for its object, the construction of a reel in such a manner that the axis of the spool or drum on which the line is wound always remains parallel to the rod to which the reel is attached, the said spool or drum remaining stationary either when "casting" or "recovering" the line in the operation of angling.

By the use of a reel constructed in accordance with my invention, better "casts" may be made owing to the decrease in friction hitherto experienced, and the line may be wound evenly on the spool or drum.

In carrying out my invention, the revolving disc of the reel is provided on or towards its outer edge with, by preference, bevel teeth, thus forming a toothed wheel, such toothed wheel engaging in turn a bevel toothed wheel which is revolubly mounted around a spindle of suitable length, such spindle being mounted and free to slide, but not to revolve, in suitable bearings attached to the plate which carries the before mentioned revolving disc. The said spindle is parallel to the rod, and one end of the same projects towards the point of the rod.

Attached to the bevel toothed wheel, is what is known to the textile trade as a "flyer" provided with one or more false eyes. On the revolving disc being operated by the angler, the bevel wheel and "flyer" will revolve around the spindle.

The spool or drum around which the line is wound is mounted on and towards the projecting end of the spindle in such a manner that the same may be retained securely thereon, and at the same time be removed therefrom when desired, but should a certain strain be placed on the line by reason of a fish being hooked, or the hook being held by weed or other matter, then the said spool or drum may revolve, the ease with which such revolution will take place being capable of regulation.

In order that the line may be evenly wound on the spool or drum, the line is passed through one of the false eyes of the "flyer", and the spindle is given a sliding motion, similar to what is known in textile industries as a "litter motion". This motion may be imparted by the angler by means of a cam, lever, or the like. The said cam or the like may be operated by means of the revolving disc, or by the thumb or finger of the angler; in the latter case, the said cam or the like is engaged by a suitable spring which will always return same to its original position.

In operation, when "casting" or "recovering" the line, the spool or drum remains stationary. When "casting" the line slips off the end of the spool.

In "recovering" the line is passed through a false eye on the "flyer" and the "flyer" revolved as before described. The spindle, together with the spool,

[Price 8d.]

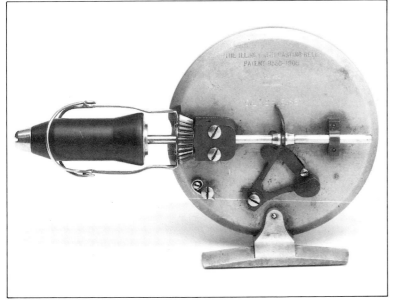

Part of the original patent taken out by Illingworth in 1905 for his 'Bait Casting Reel' BELOW: a closer view of the reel itself.

Simple Proceedure – When a cork backing is due simply hook the bait to a fence and then walk away, letting out the line as you go until all is taken from the drum. The particular backing then to be inserted is governed by the length of the line to be cut away. Tie the line to it and wind up the line, walking as you do so to the fence. That part of the line which the drum will not accommodate is the worn part. Throw it away and refix the bait.

Tensions on the Spool, Two Ways of Regulating It – The tension is regulated in accordance with the strength of the line employed and of the quarry pursued. The means of regulation is a pointer or switch moved from indent to indent. There are seven on the face of the spool. If the varying tensions thus afforded are not sufficient, a tension washer must be added to those already operating between the spool and the face of the reel. The reel literally, and as the phrase goes, speaks for itself through the medium of a one-way tong and ratchet. Thus all notice is given by it to the angler when a fish is taking line as a warning to cease the application of pressure when there should be no pressure.

The Reel can be Manipulated by either the Right or Left Hand – The reel winds anticlockwise and the left hand is generally used, but should any angler find it difficult in using his left hand for this purpose the rod can be turned after casting to bring the reel upwards and the right hand used for winding, which of course, necessitates changing the rod from the right to the left hand.

For Float Fishing as well as for Spinning – The

ABOVE AND RIGHT: *a very rare threadline casting reel, reputedly Illingworth's first prototype. The brass gears and cam are built into the body of a 2³⁄₄in. bronzed brass trout reel with bone handle on the winding arm. The turned wooden bobbin spool with brass backplate, triangular brass clutch plate and brass tension nut are all mounted on a brass cam-driven shaft, working through the axle of the revolving, double-hooked, brass retrieving arm, 2³⁄₄in. by 6¹⁄₂in. Illingworth was working on his designs for a threadline reel between 1903 and 1904 and the first one was built from his drawings by a Mr More. Writing in 1907, Illingworth states that he had had three season's use out of it, and that some of his friends were trying out others. No mention is made of how many Mr More had made, or if there had been any refinements, but it was probably only a very few for Illingworth's close friends to assist in trials.*

Illingworth reel was designed primarily for trout spinning or for similar work, but salmon of great weight have been taken by it. It is excellent for grayling, perch and jack fishing and as a means of throwing a float great distances when coarse fishing.

Easy to Use – It will, after a little practice, be found that the manipulation of the Illingworth reel becomes automatic. It is placed with the handle on the left side of the rod and the line is retrieved by turning the handle anticlockwise with the left hand. When holding the rod, the second finger of the right hand should press against the pillar to which the spool and the gear are mounted. This position of the hand permits free play to the fore-finger to pick up the line after the bait has been thrown. The line should be smartly drawn into the corner of angle formed by the bottom of rod grip and reel pillar. It is then caught by the revolving flyer, which is immediately put into motion by turning the handle. Remove the finger just as soon as the eye in the fly catches the line and proceeed to wind the line onto the spool. When the line is thus retrieved, it should be removed from the eye of the flyer preparatory to a cast in the following manner: Pick up the line in the way already described and disengage it from the eye of the flyer by revolving the handle in the backward direction, i.e., towards yourself. The line will then rest near the first joint of the finger. Extend the finger and let the line travel on to its tip, and in the act of making the cast straighten the finger to its full extent in order that the line may easily slip from it.

The Illingworth reel retailed for about £4 12s 6d and was the major innovation of the fixed spool spinning reel that was to last into modern times.

An Illingworth No. 3 casting reel.

Undoubtedly one of the great classics among British reels was the Aeriel made by Allcock's at their Standard Works at Redditch. This reel made its first appearance on the market in 1896 and was then known as the Coxon Aeriel Reel, later to be known as the Allcock Aeriel. This famous reel remained in production, with few alterations, for about 60 years, in fact until the demise of the company in the 1960s. The Aeriel became one of the longest lasting and most important reels for the coarse fisherman in this century.

The Aeriel was one of the most significant developments of the basic Nottingham reel, and indeed was the brainchild of a Nottingham angler and champion caster, H. Coxon. The Coxon Aeriel shot to fame at the International Angler's

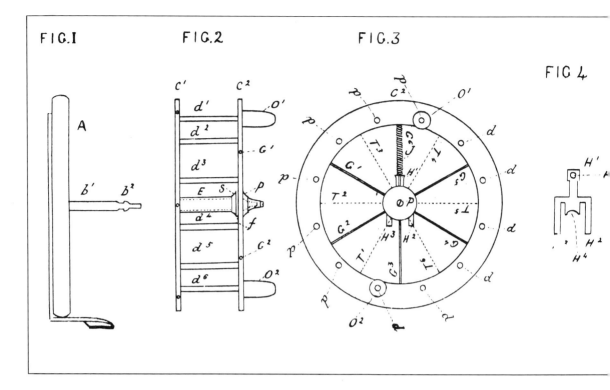

FIG.I   FIG.2   FIG.3   FIG 4

Tournament at Wimbledon in 1896, when Mr Coxon won both the Barbel and the Chubb Float Casting Championships with a single longest cast of 81 feet 6 inches.

Coxon's Aeriel was revolutionary in its phenomenal lightness and freedom of action. While the drum of a normal centre-pin reel weighed 4 ounces at this time and required a certain amount of force to set it in motion, the drum of the Aeriel weighed only 1¾ ounces and could be set in motion by the merest breath. Each revolution of the drum let out or took in 9 inches of line. The lightness was achieved by constructing the revolving portion, or drum, merely with two ebonite hoops connected by light metal bars. Constructed on the spider principle, the line wound around the bars, leaving the centre exposed to the air. Original models had wooden back plates, which were later replaced by alloy back plates; the reel was thus excellent for use in damp conditions, since it allowed the line some opportunity to dry. Drying was also helped by the high-speed revolution of the drum, which acted as an in-built fan.

The Fishing Gazette, reviewing the reel later in 1896 commented that it was 'the lightest reel we have ever seen'. However, the writer foresaw reservations on the part of those anglers not used to the Trent style of fishing and who might

Part of the patent details of the Ariel reel, dated 1896.

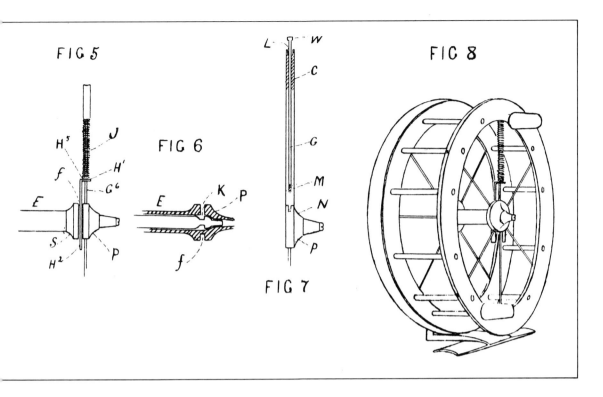

FIG 5

FIG 6

FIG 7

FIG 8

ask, 'What is the object of having a reel which spins like a top? An ordinary Nottingham reel is quite hard enough to manage.' Allcock's took note of the point and provided a range with an adjustable check.

By the time of publication of the 1937/8 catalogue the reel had become known as the Allcock Aeriel, and the name of Coxon had been dropped. In that catalogue the reel was referred to as 'a beautiful example of the reel maker's art', and Allcock's were prepared to guarantee the materials and the mechanism from faults of workmanship without time limit. The makers regarded it as an excellent general-purpose reel, suitable for spinning, fly fishing and float fishing. When used for spinning, and this is where the Aeriel excelled, the drum was controlled by pressure of a finger or thumb on the rim of the drum.

The 'Improved Model' was described as being made of aluminiunim, but with a dull bronze anti-corrosive finish, perforated front rim, patent drag adjustable to any tension according to the weight of bait, optional lever ratchet check on rim, ample line capacity and white xylonite handles. In the 1930s it was made in three sizes: 3½ inch at 53s 6d; 4 inch at 57s and 4½ inch at 63s 6d.

Allcock's also produced a number of thread line fishing

reels, on much the same lines as the Illingworth examples. There was to be no diminution in demand for the reels variously known as light casting, fixed spool or thread line reels . These reels were intended for casting ultra-light baits direct from the reel either for coarse fishing or spinning and there was no danger of overrunning. Their use permitted the angler to choose the lightest of tackle without the hazard of breakage, providing that the water was free of weeds or other obstruction. The slip-in clutch acted as a buffer when a large fish pulled suddenly and prevented undue strain on the fine line by giving out a certain amount of line even though the angler might be winding in. A light bait, such as a minnow or prawn, could be cast without difficulty in spinning for salmon, pike or especially trout, while the coarse fisherman could cast float tackle of up to three drams 90 feet or more, straight from the reel. A cast of this distance brought within range many fish that would normally be out of reach. A tendency to kinking of the line and the reels' unsuitability in weed-infested waters were their principle drawbacks.

During the 1920s and until the company's closure in the mid-thirties, the three main thread line reels which Allcock's promoted were:

Felton Cross Wind — 'A beautifully made winch' for salmon, sea trout, pike, marcia, bass etc — in fact for the fish which would require lines of up to 15 pounds breaking strain, or conditions where weeds would provide a hazard for lighter lines.

Duplex — particularly for spinning, but also for bottom fishing. It was recommended especially for shallow stream fishing as it enabled the line to be retrieved very rapidly before it had time to become snagged on the bottom.

Allcock Stanley — 'A wonderful little reel at a remarkably low price'. The Stanley was a light casting reel recommended for general coarse fishing, occasional spinning and, especially, for float fishing.

The Allcock Stanley was a remarkably popular reel for a number of years. Glowing testimonials were published in the catalogues. One angler landed a 16lb 8oz pike in just 20 minutes and another a 14lb 10oz carp on the Florida Lake near Johannesburg. One testimonial is especially noteworthy: 'It may interest you to hear that I caught a salmon weighing 14lb 8ozs on a light caster rod and your Allcock's Stanley Reel. It took exactly 35 minutes to kill the fish . . . I also caught a number of sea trout, the best being just under 3lbs. I am delighted with the tackle especially as I am an absolute novice in the art of fishing!'

The photograph highlights the huge range in sizes of reels. The larger is the 'Mitchell Henry' big game reel and the smaller is an early nineteenth-century brass pole winch. The latter is a free-running winch, but features a sliding latch mounted on the pillars which, when engaged, prevents the handle from rotating.

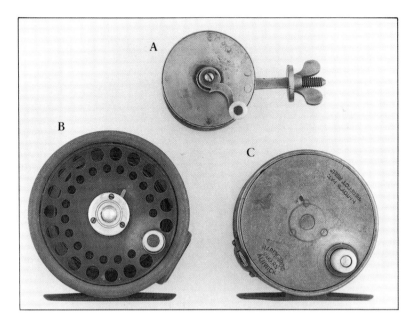

A: *a brass spike-footed reel, 1½ in. diameter and 1½ in. wide.* B: *a Hardy 'St George' trout-fly reel.* C: *a Hardy 2⅝ in. wide drum Perfect reel (stamped 'Hardy's Patent Perfect Reel').*

The popularity of the Allcock Stanley is hard to explain. It is of an unusual design, and therefore will be of interest to the collector as a curiosity. But for use it could hardly compare with other Allcock reels, the Illingworth range or the Hardy Hardex and Altex reels. Perhaps its comparatively low price of 25 shillings in 1937 endeared it to many anglers, especially the absolute novice!

No general work on this vast subject can hope to cover all the reels made by the host of manufacturers that sprang into being with the increased demand for tackle in the last hundred years. The reels so far described, with the important exception of those by Hardy Brothers which are covered in their own chapter, represent the major developments. This is not to say that other reels are of no interest to the collector. Quite the contrary, numerous reels were made by less well-known makers, which fulfilled specific requirements of the time without becoming influential in the general progress of the reel, but which are of great interest to the collector on account of their rarity and, in some cases, their peculiarity.

A fine example of a named and dated mid nineteenth-century salmon reel by Eaton & Deller. The winding arm carries the inscription 'Registered Dec. 1856'.

CHAPTER THREE

American reels

AMERICA has a long and distinguished tradition of reel manufacture. For almost two centuries American reels have been comparable to anything made elsewhere.

The reels of the eighteenth century, to judge from the few survivals, were the equivalents of the simple 'winches' then being used in Britain. It is more than likely that early settlers would have equipped themselves in Europe before setting out for the New World. However, there were several factors which contributed to the growth of an independent American reel manufacturing industry.

From the early years of the nineteenth century settlers pushed farther west and discovered lakes and rivers stocked with fish unfamiliar to Europeans. Although the indigenous Indian population had fished these waters from time immemorial, they had in no way been over-exploited in the way many British fishing grounds were to be. Nor did they suffer, at that time, from pollution from industrial waste, then becoming a problem in Europe. Somewhat at odds with the popular image of the settlers in the North American states and in Canada being perpetually at war with the Indian population, there are records of fishing parties led by well-known Indian guides in the 1830s and 1840s. In fact the first Indian recorded as casting a fly was Tome Cope, a Nova Scotian Micmac, who cast to Atlantic salmon in 1839. The settlers, both Americans pushing farther west and the European newcomers were, of necessity, hardy outdoor types equally at ease with a rod as with a gun. It is perhaps no coincidence that the Blue Grass country of Kentucky, one of the richest agricultural and sporting areas in America, originated the Kentucky rifle, one of the most refined muzzle-loaded sporting rifles, as well as the Kentucky bait-casting reel. The latter was to become to the Americans what the Nottingham reel was to the British, the basis from which many important developments grew.

There is no doubt that many immigrants would have brought with them their own tried and trusted reels. They would also have had available to them basic brass winches imported from England. But the special conditions they encountered soon led to the creation of the first truly

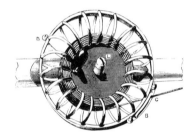

The Follett winch of the late 1880s.

A late nineteenth-century decorated crank-handled brass trout reel. The winding and back plates of this reel are embossed with a figure of an angler pursuing his sport. The decoration is the main point of interest, as the rod is of a very basic construction.

American reel. Little is known about the personal lives of the early reel smiths. However, George Snyder is generally credited with making the first multiplying reel for use in bass fishing. Snyder was a watchmaker by trade, living and working in Kentucky in the first quarter of the nineteenth century. Clearly he was a man of exceptional resource who spotted the potential demand for precision-made reels which his technical skill and equipment could create. The precision of the watchmaker, brought to the manufacture of reels, set a standard which placed the Kentucky Reel of the nineteenth century among the finest in the world. Consequently these reels are among the most desirable when they occasionally appear on the market. As will be seen this was not to be the first occasion when horology was to have a significant effect on the production of American reels. It is interesting that a writer for the magazine *Spirit*, on 15th June 1850 makes a direct comparison between the two crafts:

An early twentieth-century fly reel, the 'Rainbow' by A.E. Meisselbach. It is fitted to a contemporary rod called 'The Devine Rainbow'.

RIGHT: *A size 5/0, vom Hofe multiplying sea reel of ebonite and nickel silver, with counterbalance handle. The front plate is marked with the patent dates 1885, 1889 and 1902.*

A good example of a vom Hofe salmon reel, showing the fine work executed by the maker, and underlining how desirable these reels are to the collector.

Julius vom Hofe. A hard rubber and nickel silver multiplying reel by one of the leading reel manufacturers of America. The name vom Hofe is synonymous with the very highest standards of fishing tackle manufacture.

. . . the birth of an A., No.1 multiplier is as important as the making of a first quality gold watch. The brass which should be cast, must be pure metal, new and entirely free from sand holes; the case, box or spool, handle wheel and all flat parts, should be hammered to their utmost tension without cracking and if thoroughly hammered will ring like a bell. The pillars and screws should be drawn from the best wire, without annealing as hard as possible; so that they shall file almost like steel; drawn tempered and polished after the same method as finest watch work. The teeth of the wheel and pinions should be of large size and capable of resisting almost any pressure. They should be truly cut, polished and finished with the most acute correctness. The cutting depends much on the machine used. None but skilful mechanics can make and put together such a reel and only the most scientific angler should use one.

Reels such as described are made with stops that push and pull much like an organ, tightly and evenly fitted so that no room is allowed for the least bit of moisture, and are far superior to the old English side moving stop, which leaves space for the collection of everything which injures a perfect running reel. They are also made with a drag. As proof of their perfect strength, capacity and durability, I will cite for 'Dinks' and his 'anti-multiplier friends' that there is now in the possession of four professional bass and salmon fishing friends four reels made in 1837. Two of the fishers are men of leisure and have angled on fresh or salt water three or six days every week. Mr. P., the owner of one, on an excursion to the Denny's River in Maine, 1841, took a salmon that weighed 17½ pounds; the fish on the first run taking out two hundred and fifty feet of line. He was beautifully managed and taken without the least bit of difficulty.

One of the most popular and numerous of the sporting fish in North America is the bass. The name is a corruption of the old English word 'barse' or the German 'bars' for various species of the sea and freshwater perch. A colloquial name for the English perch is 'sea-wolf' which gives some indication of its aggressive nature. While the European perch can grow up to about 15 pounds, the North American bass frequently weighs-in at about 25 to 30 pounds. This voracious fish feeds off smaller fish, so the bait has to be cast and drawn in at great speed in imitation of a small fish. Snyder's multiplying reel was the best available aid to catching this fast, hard fighting fish. The angler was able to wind in four times as much line at the turn of the handle on a multiplier as with the conventional centre-pin reel.

By the 1840s several Kentucky reelsmiths were in production, all making variations of the bait-casting reel. These reels were made entirely by hand and all were of excellent quality. The most notable of the early makers are: Jonathan Fleming Meek, working with his brother B.F. Meek in Frankfurt, Kentucky; Meek and Millam; and B.C. Millam somewhat later. The reels by Meek and Millam are distinctive in that all screws are numbered with corresponding numbers to each hole, an indication of the accuracy and precision of these finely engineered reels. B.F Meek later moved to Louisville where he established a small factory, with his two sons entering the business as apprentices. There a range of Blue Grass reels were made which are generally considered to be among the finest casting reels ever produced.

Contemporary with these were the reelsmiths of New York: Andrew Clark, Krider, J.C. Conroy, Shipley, and J.B. Crook & Company, making bait-casting reels with only minor variations on the Kentucky reel but of equal quality in their precision engineering.

Early American reels are generally marked with the maker's name, either stamped or engraved. However, where a reel is not so marked, attribution is difficult. Reels of distinctive type by well-known makers were frequently reproduced, often almost exactly, by skilled craftsmen who could well have been former employees of these companies.

American reels of the first generation are highly prized items for the collector. Their production was small compared to later developments and this, combined with their uniformly high quality, has rendered them scarce and among the most costly items for the collector.

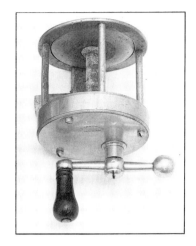

A multiplying reel of nickel silver with turned wooden handle, on a straight winding arm, with counterbalance ball weight. Made by J.B. Crook & Co, New York.

Two multiplying reels, both manufactured by J.C. Conroy, which illustrate the difference between the highly decorative presentation reel and the very simple finish of the standard model.

A plain brass multiplying reel by J.C. Conroy & Co., New York, from the mid nineteenth century. A typical feature of the New York reel makers was the brass rod with turned wooden handle and counterbalance ball.

During the third quarter of the nineteenth century the market in America for fishing tackle of all kinds expanded rapidly, concurrent with that in Europe. Methods of mass production were introduced for reels to meet the increased demand, the component parts being made by machine and finished and assembled by hand. In spite of the greater volume of output, American reels continued to maintain a high standard.

Edward vom Hofe & Company of New York, founded in 1867, were a leading manufacturing company of this period. Their range included some important fly reels, the most notable being the Perfection, Peerless, Restigouche — a single-action salmon reel named after the well-known salmon river — and the Tibique, a double-action (multiplying action) salmon reel.

One of the most significant developments in the latter years of the nineteenth century and one which had great influence on both American and British reels, was in the use of perforations, often forming a decorative motif. The main advantage of these was to reduce the weight of a metal reel, but it also allowed the line, still made of silk at this period, to dry to some extent while still on the reel. The metal cage, or skeleton reel took this advantage to its logical conclusion. As early as 1859 the Billinghurst, a fully developed skeleton reel was patented. But although (perhaps because) it was in advance of its time, despite continuing in production for many years, its following was limited. A similar reel, the Follett, which appeared in the 1880s, also met with limited success. A number of these found their way into Britain and were favourably reviewed in J. H. Keenes' *Fishing Tackle, Its Materials and Manufacture*, of 1886. The Billinghurst and especially the Follett are among the rarest of American reels.

Two other reels, similar in design to the Follett were produced in vulcanite, a particularly hard form of rubber in common use as a lightweight alternative to metal. The Fowler was patented in 1872 with the added feature of a check mechanism; the Clinton, patented in 1889, differed little from the Fowler reel, though it was illustrated in Dr James Henshall's 1904 edition of *The Book of the Black Bass*. The author of this celebrated work is said to have assembled in the 1880s what must have been one of the first great collections of early American fishing tackle, notably Kentucky reels. The fate of the collection still remains a mystery after more than 100 years.

Charles F. Orvis, if not the inventor of the perforated reel, was certainly one of the first to make it a commercial success.

The Orvis Trout Reel first appeared in 1874. It was made of nickel-plated brass and supplied in a fitted black walnut box. The distinctive feature of this reel was its narrow perforated spool: the narrow spool enabled the line to be retrieved more quickly, because the line was wound round a greater diameter than a conventional wide drum reel. The perforations allowed excess water to escape from the line and thus aided drying. Its commercial success was considerable on both sides of the Atlantic and was further developed in Britain by H. Cholmondeley-Pennell.

Indiana reels were uniquely American. They were large centre-pin reels developed for trolling in deep water lakes. Consequently, they needed to hold large quantities of line and have a free running action. They also were of ventilated metal construction and may be of simple form or fitted with an optional ratchet or brake. Indiana reels were developed at the same time as the Orvis Trout Reel; it appears unlikely that any predate 1874.

Not surprisingly, in view of the size and geographical variety of the United States, a far greater range and quantity of reels has been produced than in Britain. By 1895 tarpon fishing in the Gulf of Mexico had become popular among wealthy anglers from America and also from Europe. Alfred C. Harmsworth, writing in that year, stated that, 'As a matter of fact, all but the remote portions of Florida can be reached in nine days from London, and when one arrives at one's destination there is a capital assortment of outdoor amusements open.' Harmsworth regarded the tarpon as the king of game fish, salmon not excepted. Before 1885 no large tarpon had been caught with rod and reel until a Mr Wood

An elevation and sectional view of an Abbey and Imbrie's patent quadruple winch, showing the steel bearings (A & h) which could be adjusted to compensate for wear and also to increase the drag on the reel.

An example of Edward vom Hofe's 'Celebrated' salmon and grilse click reel, made from finest quality rubber and nickel silver. The illustration comes from the 1907 catalogue, when the company were based at 95 & 97 Fulton Street, NY. This example is a single action, size 4/0.

of New York City brought to gaff a fish of over 100 pounds. Two noted anglers of the period were Lord and Lady Orford who made regular visits to the area for the sport. In 1895 Lady Orford became probably the only woman in the world to have killed two tarpon in one day, one of them weighing 128 pounds.

Harmsworth, writing about the new sport in 1895, recommended that suitable equipment could be had from Conroy's at 310 Broadway, New York City and he records having spent £10 on his tackle. For the rod he paid 24 shillings, but £6 for the reel, and the rest on hooks and lines. He further suggested that the angler should take several rods and plenty of hooks, having himself broken a borrowed rod and split a friend's reel. He goes on to quote a piece of advice given to him by an old Southern gentleman, which his friends probably wished he had taken: 'When you buy tarpon tackle, young man, you have got to remember that you may expect to hook something like a thirty-knot torpedo boat.' Julius vom Hofe and the Cozzone company were only two among many companies who developed reels for saltwater fishing.

Towards the end of the nineteenth century the leading companies began to develop large reels for use in big game

Three variations of the famous Orvis reel, one in its original wooden case.

fishing. Later, in the 1920s, Bronson and J. A. Cox produced fine hand-made saltwater reels. William Boschen, who worked for a time at Thomas Conroy's tackle store in New York, experienced the hazards of using inadequate reels for big game fishing and the injury that could result. The handles of the reel could revolve at great speed and any contact between them and the winding hand could prove extremely painful. Boschen developed an internal drag-and-clutch mechanism, with a non-revolving handle, especially for such reels; this enabled the handle to remain stationary as the line was being taken from the spool while playing a large fish. He took his design to Julius vom Hofe of Brookline who developed the reel for production. At first the reel was considered far too complex and was even ridiculed by big game anglers. However, in 1913, when Boschen caught the first broad bill swordfish ever taken on rod and line using this reel, anglers began to take the big game reel seriously. Although, in the first decades of the century, these reels were monuments to technical prowess, under the pressure of increasing competition they became over-complicated in design, and had the fundamental disadvantage of being far too difficult to service, especially at sea. Big game reels have, since the 1930s, become more practical in design. In 1932, Hardy's of Alnwick developed a reel for the famous author Zane Grey which was a classic of its time and which has recently been reintroduced into Hardy's production.

The Orvis Pennell trout reel, showing the modified double handle, as fitted by H. Cholmondeley-Pennell.

Simplicity was the essence of one of the best known of the Heddon reels. The Heddon Company is typical of the later nineteenth century manufacturers in their wide range of reels, produced in quantities to a high standard. Established in Dowagiac, Michigan, a series of trolling, bait casting and some automatic fly reels were produced as late as the 1930s. The Heddon Early 45 Reel is especially notable for its simplicity of construction and it is a classic of its type. It incorporated a William Carter's patent of 5th July 1904 and 28th November 1905, which enabled the angler to dismantle the reel quickly and easily for servicing. The important Carter's patents are also to be found on some of the Meeks' range of reels. Heddon reels are noted not only for their high quality but also for their exceptionally high cost and it was not until the 1930s that they began to produce more competitively priced reels.

By the end of the nineteenth century angling had become popular among widely differing sections of society. The great increase in popular demand was catered for by rapidly expanding manufacturing companies using the latest mass-

V *A collection of nineteenth-century reels by Vom Hofe.*

VI *A Heddon multiplying reel, carrying the Carter's patent.*

Three versions of the 'Automatic' fly reel, produced by Yawman & Erbe of Rochdale, New York.

production methods. Among a number of familiar names, some of which are still in business, the Hendryx Company based in New Haven, Connecticut, is outstanding for its success in making large quantities of low-priced reels. Again we note a possible close connection between reel manufacture and clockmaking. It can be no coincidence that the reel production methods bear a remarkable similarity to those of the flourishing kitchen clock industry, also centred in New Haven. Both produced movements of the most basic type with parts stamped out of sheets of brass. Reels of this kind cannot be compared in quality with their expensive hand-finished counterparts, but they do have an interest to the collector in the great variety of models produced, and they also have the advantage of being plentifully available at modest cost. The Hendryx Company is reputed to have produced 248 different models and sold more than two million of them over a period of 12 years. Although such mass-produced reels may have little rarity value, they are of considerable interest to the collector. Hendryx reels are generally marked simply with the name of the company.

The Shakespeare Company of Kalamazoo, Michigan, is

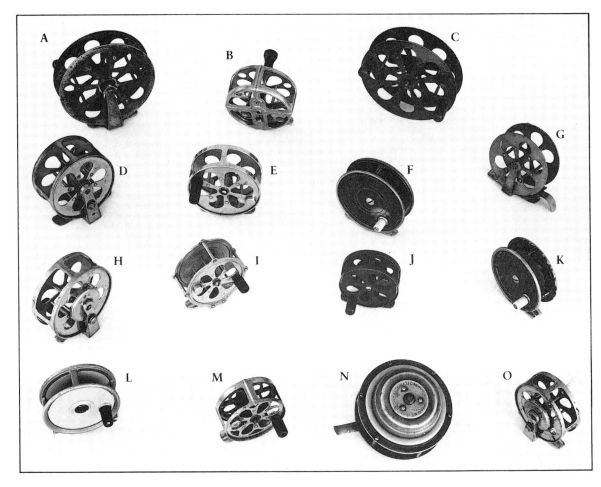

one of the major reel manufacturers of America. From its beginnings in the early years of this century, the company has produced an interesting and, in many cases, innovative range of reels. They have maintained a position in the forefront of reel development and have competed successfully with their rivals, Heddon, Horton and Pflueger.

The major American reel manufacturers of the late nineteenth and early twentieth centuries mentioned so far: the vom Hofe family, the Meeks, Heddon, Shakespeare, and Hendryx, together with Meisselbach, Horton and Pflueger, have all produced extensive ranges of reels and the choice for the collector is vast. The field might be narrowed to any one of these companies and the collector could still assemble a representative selection of the innovations and standard models available to anglers during these decades.

A range of Meisselbach reels.
A: *trolling reel;* **B:** *'Featherlight';*
C: *trolling reel;* **D:** *wide 'Expert' with exposed check;* **E:** *'Expert' reel;* **F:** *'Rainbow' No. 631;*
G: *'Expert' type with thumb drag, c.1890;* **H:** *'Expert' with circular check housing;* **I:** *'Allright' reel;*
J: *'Expert' No. 19;* **K:** *'Rainbow' c.1925, No. 62;* **L:** *believed to be an 'Airey Meisselbach';*
M: *'Featherlight';* **N:** *the first Meisselbach 'Automatic', 1914;*
O: *'Expert' No 19, c.1886.*

CHAPTER FOUR

Flies and related equipment

THE USE OF FLIES for the purpose of catching fish dates back at least 2,000 years, although there is only minimal documentary evidence to support this prior to the fifteenth century. The Roman writer, Claudius Aelian, refers to the Macedonians toiling on the banks of the River Astracus, between Berea and Thessalonica, to catch fish with a fly named Hippurus. He describes this fly as a very singular insect, marked like a wasp, the size of a hornet and having the buzz of a bee. It was the favourite food of the anglers' quarry. The Macedonians did not take the trouble to catch quantities of the Hippurus and simply impale them on a hook, but copied and tied a basic model of the insect, using for the body a purple wool and attaching a pair of waxy, coloured wings. Nor was the fly hurled indiscriminately on to the water and allowed to sink. The fishermen let the fly drop gently on to the surface and drift downstream in the natural way for the fish to rise and take a 'dainty bait', in what appears to be a very early form of dapping. This is a method associated with loch fishing that requires a long rod. The wind catches the line which in turn lifts the fly on and off the surface of the water. No casting is involved.

The first angling manual appeared in 1496 as part of the celebrated *Boke of St Albans* by the somewhat enigmatic figure, Dame Juliana Berners, reputed to be the prioress of Sopwell. The *Boke* was a collection of treatises on hawking, hunting and heraldry, adapted into verse from a translation of an earlier work, *Art of Hunting* by Guillaume Twiti, Huntsman to Edward II. Although the text is signed by Dame Juliana little else appears to be known about her. The book was one of the many which were published at the Caxton Press in Westminster by Wynkyn de Worde at the end of the fifteenth century. Included in it was the 'Treatise of Fysshynge with an Angle', a section of which deals with 'Fishing for Rising Trout with a Dubbe', a dubbe being an archaic term for a fly. Directions are given for twelve patterns of flies for trout and grayling, most of which would not be

From The Boke of Hawkyng Huntynge and Fysshyng *by Dame Juliana Berners.*

entirely useless today. One example is the doone fly, the body of which is made of a dun-coloured wool and the wings of partridge feather. Another doone fly had a body of black wood and wings of 'blackest drake and jay' with a tail of the same colour.

Flies are among the most decorative items for the tackle collector and look well when displayed in a frame. They are to the fly fisherman what the float is to the coarse fisherman. Both collectors and fishermen tend to be fascinated by their beauty and collect far more than they need. The many hundreds of examples currently available to the fly fisherman are probably responsible for catching as many anglers as fish. Flies are, however, among the most ephemeral of the angler's tackle, being used a few times, possibly for a whole season, and then lost or worn out and discarded. Early examples are, therefore, difficult to find in good condition. For this reason the earliest available are likely to be no earlier than from the end of the nineteenth century. Numerous companies produced large ranges of flies of many kinds and assembled display frames showing the various types. Although these are scarce on the market they are highly desirable; many collectors concentrate on one particularly well-known tyer, and the works of living craftsmen are keenly sought. Women have long been famous for their dexterity in tying flies. A reviewer of the Fisheries Exhibition in 1896 commented that the wife of J. R. Richardson, a well-known tackle manu-facturer, was an expert fly tyer and had been brought up in the business. She could be seen on their stand tying flies to order, and her speciality was a mayfly named 'Queen of the May', which had light lemon wings.

At the same exhibition Messers Ogden Smith were commended for a grand selection of mayflies, including ten

Types of early nineteenth-century salmon flies and hooks.

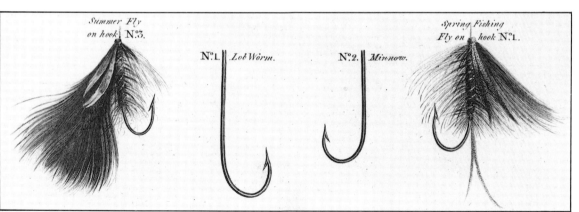

different shades of the spent mayfly 'The Gladstone', and small dry flies both on gut and on eyed hooks. A single good-quality skin of the Egyptian Goose cost as much as 50s. The trout flies with small spinners at the head, to be found on the stand of Carter and Company, were considered 'regular poaching affairs if used on any water where fly fishing only is allowed, unquestionably very deadly'.

Old flies have become scarce because of their fragile nature: they are very susceptible to moth and the rusting of the hooks has often been the cause of damage. Until fairly recently, before the collector's interest had raised the level of the value of an old fly, it was usual for a good example to be taken apart and the best material reused; particularly so when certain material had become scarce, such as the feathers of the Jungle Cock, used in salmon and some trout flies. The capes of this bird were exported from its native India until the 1960s, when it became a protected species, and a ban on its import was imposed. The bird is now being bred in Britain and so supplies are again available to the tyer, but at high cost. In a similar instance, when the Vulterine Guinea Fowl bacame a protected species, its feathers became unavailable for a time for tying the Blue Elver salmon fly. No way could be found to provide a satisfactory substitute until the bird began to be bred especially for the purpose. Not surprisingly, the feathers of the Condor are no longer available for tying certain of the nymph patterns for which they had been particularly suited, although in this case very good alternatives are used.

The tools and equipment of the fly tyer were of the most basic and could be found in any house. The main piece of equipment used by the modern tyer is the vice, but this is a comparatively recent innovation of the late nineteenth century, used to hold the hook while tying the fly. Before that time the hook was simply held in the fingers, and for many years into this century the professional tyers disdained the use of the vice. A typical tool kit of the late nineteenth century would have comprised a pricker, known today as a dubbing needle, a pair of sharp pointed scissors and a pair of spring tweezers as an early form of hackle plyer.

The materials were many and varied, and to some extent

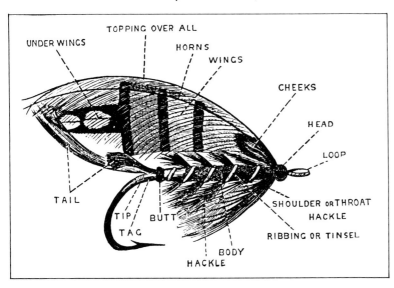

An engraving from Fishing *by H. Cholmondeley Pennell, showing the different parts of a salmon-fly.*

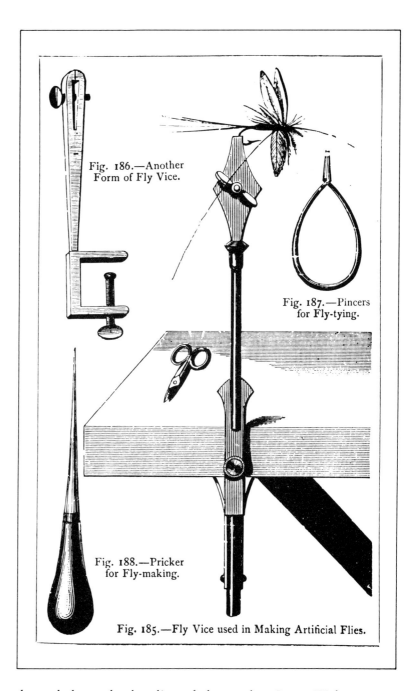

Fig. 186.—Another Form of Fly Vice.

Fig. 187.—Pincers for Fly-tying.

Fig. 188.—Pricker for Fly-making.

Fig. 185.—Fly Vice used in Making Artificial Flies.

A selection of late Victorian fly tying tools.

depended on the locality of the angler. Izaac Walton went into great detail as to the most suitable furs and feathers to use and even suggested pieces of old Turkey carpet! In describing how to tie a fly he commented: 'I confess, no direction can be given to make a man of dull capacity able to make a fly well; and yet I know this, with a little practice, will help an ingenious angler in a good degree; but to see a fly made by an artist in that kind, is the best teaching to make it.' He goes on to recommend to the 'ingenious angler' that, while walking along the river bank, he might observe the type of fly which is attracting the fish. He should catch a specimen and, out of his store of bear's hair, feathers, wool and thread (all kept in a parchment wallet which he also describes how to make) quickly make precisely the fly which will ensure the most encouraging success. An ingenious angler, indeed, but by no means unknown today.

The materials have varied little over a very long period of time and even now many of the traditional elements are still used and only varied by the need to find substitutes. Walton recommended various hair which could be suitable — bear, camel, and badger hair, and spaniel's hair taken from behind the ear — and was specific as to colour. Hog's down might be had from the butcher about Christmas and must be plucked from under the throat. Seal fur, to be had at the trunkmaker's since it was commonly used to cover the typical dome-topped travelling trunks, was greatly to be preferred to that of cow or calf, which were too hard and 'never work kindly, nor lay handsomely'. The furrier might also be required to supply suitable tufts of fox or otter (to be either old animals or cubs), squirrel, badger, fulimart (foumart or polecat), hare ('from the neck where it is the colour of withered fern'), and the yellow fur of the marten.

Walton also suggested various fabrics which 'will furnish excellent Dubbing' (covering for the body). Apart from the old piece of Turkey carpet already mentioned, mohair and camlet would do. Camlet was a fabric woven from Angora hair, or from a wool or silk substitute. One fabric he mentions, but no longer available, was barge sail which, when old and seasoned by the continuous smoke from the fire and steam from the beef kettle, would make excellent dubbing. As these sails were made of sheep's wool, the tendency for the wool to become sodden on contact with the water could be avoided by adding seal hair for small flies, and hog wool for large ones.

Feathers have always been an essential element of the well-dressed fly and have been taken from both wild and domestic birds. Feathers from all parts of the bird are used according to the appropriate colour and marking and hackles are an especially important type; these are the long, slender feathers that hang down from the head of a cock.

A reviewer of one of the important fishing exhibitions at the end of the nineteenth century commented on the display

A Forrest & Sons display board for the 1883 Fisheries Exhibition, held in London. Items similar to this, in good condition, are a rare find.

of George E. Holland of Devon. Holland was noted for the best class of trout fly but had 'recently taken it into his head to start salmon fly dressing and bid fair to hold his own in this department'. He charged two shillings for a salmon fly on a two inch hook, and had some olive, red and ginger spent quill gnats, 'which look very killing'. Retailers such as Holland commonly offered whole skins of birds for self-tying, and he was reported as having 'some grand skins of furnace, honey dun, ginger, red, badger and blue dun hackles, all from game cocks shown on behalf of Mr J. Rowe, fishing tackle maker of High Street, Barnstaple'. At that time game cocks were plentiful in the west country, and high-quality natural capes and skins were popular among fly tyers. Now they are hard to come by and dyed substitutes are generally used.

The dying of feathers, fur and hair has long been common practice when a particular shade has been required but not available naturally. Colours to suit every type of water in every kind of weather condition resulted in a large repertoire of recipes. Although the modern angler can choose from a vast array of commercially made flies, their colours are not

79

A fine oak fly case by Farlow & Co., containing four trays of flies, the whole contained in a fitted leather carrying case.

always exactly as he might wish. Therefore many anglers still take the trouble to assemble their own flies from materials they prepare themselves, but most might balk at preparing their own dyes, preferring instead to choose from the range of modern proprietory alternatives. The following old recipes are included here not just as part of the history of fly tying, but also as a testament to the ingenious lengths to which anglers will go to achieve success. This recipe for 'best yellow dye' was published in Daniel's *Rural Sports* of 1807:

The best Yellow dye for all materials for *artificial* flies, is the Bark from branches of a Crab-tree, taken in the spring

80

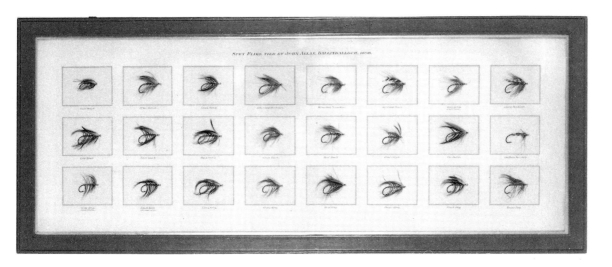

Spey flies tied by the notable John Allan of Ballindalloch.

when the *sap* is up. Before using it, put any quantity wanted into a vessel; just cover it with a mixture of one half *hard* water, and the other half *urine*, and let it stand twenty-four hours; then put it into a proper vessel, with some *alum*, so that it simmer over a slow fire about two hours: mix all well together, and take out the bark; then put in the Feathers, &c., and stir them round until the liquor just *begins to boil*; then take them out, and instantly throw them into some *hard* cold water, with a little *alum* dissolved in it; wash them out, and dry them for use. The shades of this colour may be made to vary, by dissolving more or less of the Bark, or letting the articles be in the dye a longer or shorter time.

Any angler wishing to follow such an authentic method to achieve his results should either live alone or have an unusually tolerant spouse.

Keene also refers to Blacker, a celebrated fly-tier of the mid-nineteenth century, from Soho in London, who had published a few recipes of his own. The following one is recommended for preparing a blue dye for feathers:

. . . fill a pipkin with soft water, put it on a slow fire, and add a teaspoonful of paste blue. Stir it well; and when it is more than lukewarm take a teaspoonful of cold water, drop into it twelve drops of oil of vitriol, put this in your blue dye and then put in quarter ounce of pig's wool or mohair, previously cleaned in the alum mordant. Boil it slowly for fifteen minutes, take it out with a piece of wood, and immerse in a pan of cold water. "Dry your stuff, and your colour will be fine". . .

For Claret Dye. — There is considerable difficulty in getting a natural claret; a tint so essential to such flies as the Turkey Brown — grand killer during height of summer. Add first to the Brazil-wood half the above quantity of logwood, and in the second boiling put in a piece of copperas the size of a pea, with a bit of pearl-ash the size of a nut. Boil it one hour. Cool the water, in all cases, before putting in the oil of vitriol.

To Dye Feathers Black. — Water as before. Boil two handfuls of logwood one hour; add a little sumach and elder bark. Boil these ingredients half an hour, and put in your feathers for half an hour. Take them out, cool your liquor, dissolve a bit of copperas the size of a Spanish nut and put it in your liquor adding a little argill and soda. Boil

An interesting illustration of methods of splicing and whipping, together with other items relevant to the early nineteenth-century angler.

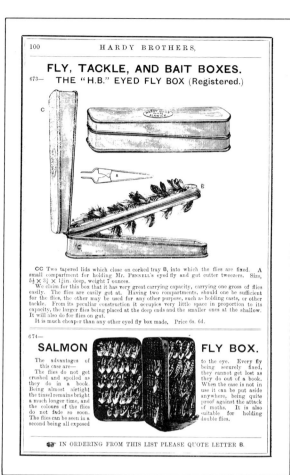

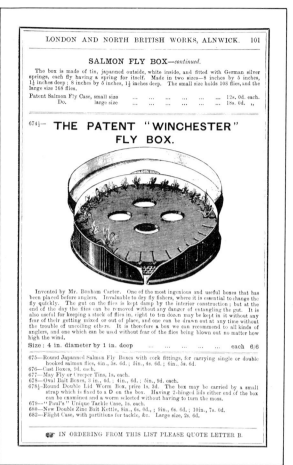

for half an hour; taking out the materials occasionally, as the air contributes to the colour, and your black will be the colour of the raven's feather.

Even at this time commercial dyes were available as an alternative to the more laborious processes described above. In all cases, however, it was recommended that prior to dying, the feathers should be boiled in a solution of alum to remove the natural grease.

The various components of the fly were tied together with silk thread, and this was coated in a fine wax to preserve it from deterioration. Some anglers used cobblers' wax but the impurities in this type of wax could result in staining. The following recipe is for a pure white wax which will not impair the colour of the silk:

Take 4ozs of the best white resin, ½oz. of fresh lard, ¼oz. of white wax. Crush the resin, and let it melt in a jar over a slow fire, stirring it all the time with a stick. Add the white wax and then the lard. Let it simmer for a quarter of an hour, then pour it out into a basin of cold water and knock it well with the hands until pliable, putting it for half an hour before the fire. Cut it into small pieces and keep in the water.

Hooks had mostly been made in London, but following the plague in 1665, the hook makers, in common with many others, left the city and the industry later re-formed in Redditch in Worcestershire. Up to the latter part of the nineteenth century hooks were usually made without an eye, and it was therefore necessary for the tyer to make an eye, using either a piece of bristle or a piece of lute gut tied on to the shank of the hook. However, many early anglers, especially those fishing for trout, tied their flies directly on to a length of gut, dispensing with the loop in favour of a more streamlined effect.

'Pocket box' for eyed trout (Bowness)

Eyed trout-fly box (Farlow)

Anglers were equipped with a pouch or wallet in which to carry their selection of flies. Walton describes in detail how such a wallet, with a number of compartments, could be made of parchment, but others were available in leather. The wallet was the most practical method of carrying flies at that time, for each fly would have a length of gut or hair line permanently attached, which could easily be looped around and carried in such a wallet. By the time of publication of Hardy's 1888 catalogue these had become known as books. There were several types available but all were generally made of leather with straps around to enclose them. The pockets were often of parchment and there might also be a number of flannel 'leaves' for drying used flies. Most books were six to seven inches in length but larger ones were also available. The normal price was in the region of 3s 6d, but one presentation book by Hardy's contained a selection of 48 different patterns of trout fly with three of each pattern, and was priced at 25 shillings. A de luxe version was made of alligator skin with four large concertina pockets, keepers for ten dozen flies, four felt leaves and other additonal items for a large quantity of flies and small associated tackle. It was regarded as the handsomest and best fitted book ever made and cost 25 shillings for a 7 inch model, 27s 6d for 7½ inch, and 30 shillings for the 8 inch.

Mr Ashley Dodd's double-eyed hook salmon-fly box (Farlow)

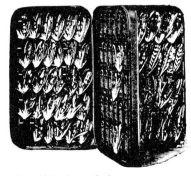

'Portable' salmon-fly box (Malloch)

The general adoption of the eyed fly hook by the end of the nineteenth century brought about a change in the method of carrying flies. No longer trailing a length of gut, it became more convenient to carry flies in a japanned block tin. These were of fairly standard pattern and varied little from one manufacturer to another. They were normally rectangular, but could be square or circular, and the interiors were normally white enamel and fitted according to the size of fly for which they were intended. Most were lined, either with cork or felt, into which the fly was hooked. Tins for salmon flies were fitted with hook clips and perhaps an extra leaf containing further clips. Many of the circular boxes were fitted with discs or small parchment trays to carry flies on gut.

Fly boxes used to be much more readily available to the collector than is now the case, and of course the named examples are usually the most desirable. When it does occur, and often on boxes made by Wheatly, which was the largest

A selection of nineteenth-century fly boxes.

The 'Latham' cast box
(F.T. Williams)

The 'Combination' salmon-fly box (Farlow)

'Double Safety' cast and fly box (Farlow)

'Test' eyed trout-fly and cast box (Farlow)

Eyed may-fly box

'Safety' cast box (Farlow)

Box for holding flies and casts (Farlow)

Safety cast and fly box

The 'Excelsior' salmon-fly box (Farlow)

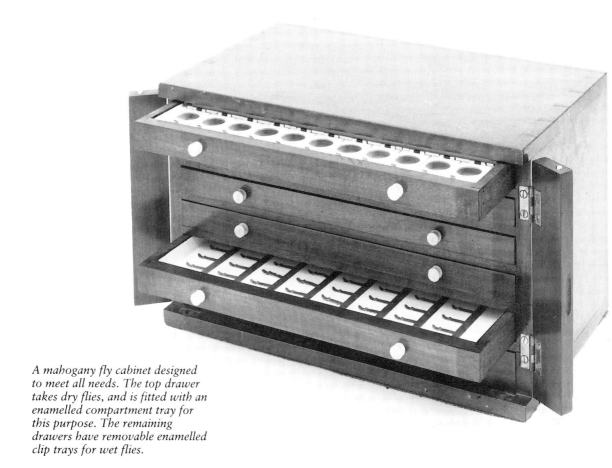

A mahogany fly cabinet designed to meet all needs. The top drawer takes dry flies, and is fitted with an enamelled compartment tray for this purpose. The remaining drawers have removable enamelled clip trays for wet flies.

The Roxburgh fly cabinet by Hardy's. The cabinet is of teak construction with four matching trays and brass furnishings.

manufacturing company, the name is either stamped into the metal or borne on an applied brass disc at the front of the box. Fine-quality boxes or books can occasionally be found with the name of the original owner inscribed on them for presentation, and may even, but rarely, contain the patterns first supplied with them. The types of fly will reveal much about the angler's own predilection and perhaps his locality. The grandest of all fly boxes are those that were not intended to be carried by the river but contained the avid angler's entire stock of salmon fly patterns in a series of compartmented drawers, from which a small selection would be made for each trip. These 'reservoirs' as they are called can be of japanned metal or mahogany and other woods. They generally date from no earlier than about 1890 and were made as late as 1930, and some of the finest, such as the 'Roxburgh' by Hardy's, are beautiful pieces of miniature cabinet making.

Fly books and, especially, boxes are very durable, and many specialist fly collectors like to include them in their collections for use as well as interest.

VII *A collection of nineteenth-century tackle.*

VIII *Bait tins, a worm box and gentle shute.*

CHAPTER FIVE

Accessories

It may seem strange to classify lines among accessories for, together with rods, they are fundamentally important to the angler. From the modern collector's point of view, however, they belong in this category. Apart from the purely practical consideration that few early lines have survived to be available to the collector, they can hardly compare with other items for decorative value. However, the technical skill required to produce this complex item makes it of at least historical importance. From the seventeenth to the end of the nineteenth century, lines were mainly of two types: those made of horse hair and those of silkworm gut, but silk, various yarns, mixed materials and even grass, are known.

Hair lines were the first on the scene. The hairs were taken from the tail of a stallion, preferably white or grey because the pale colour appeared virtually transparent in the water. They were made entirely by hand and the procedure was both laborious and time consuming. Daniel's *Rural Sports*, published in the early nineteenth century gives a good idea of the standards required to produce a good hair line. The hairs were to be sorted singly and the largest, roundest, and those which were as free from blemish as possible, were to be made up into small bundles. Having been graded by size and quality, the bundles were parcelled up and placed in clean spring water for twelve hours for a thorough washing. They were then dried with bran or simply hung in a warm room or in the sun, but too much heat would make the hairs brittle. Washed and dried, the hairs were re-sorted in bundles of about 100, with the roots aligned, and tied with thread at both ends and in the middle. They were then stored, wrapped in parchment to protect from contact with oil or grease. Hairs not immediately used for line making were dipped into water every two or three months and again dried to preserve them for a number of years.

Individual hairs were made into 'links' by twisting a selected number together. This was usually achieved by means of a line-winder or 'machine' which was available at most tackle shops for those anglers who wished to make their own lines. The line-winder described in Daniel's *Rural Sports* of 1802 had remained unchanged when Keene described it

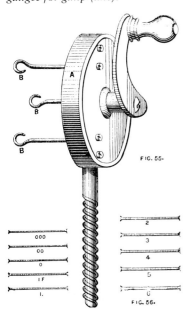

'Apparatus for twisting gut' and gauges for gimp (line).

again in 1896. The 'machine' was made of either wood or metal, usually brass, and comprised a large horizontal wheel with three small ones, enclosed in a brass box, 2 inches in diameter and ¼ inch thick. The axle of each of the small wheels extended through the underside of the box and terminated in a hook. The winder could be fixed to a post with a strong screw or clamp and was set in motion by means of a small winch in the centre of the box.

The hairs selected for each link, and these could be varied to produce a tapered line, were divided into three groups. Each group was tied with twine at one end and fixed to the three hooks and the loose ends were attached to a lead weight. The groups were evenly spaced by means of a cork, cut with three grooves, and inserted between the groups while the handle was gently turned. The cork was pushed slowly upwards until the link was completed and then removed. The ends were knotted off and stored in cold water while the process was repeated, until as many links as were needed for a line had been completed.

A fine example of a beechwood line drier stamped 'Brevete + 14955, SGDG'.

Not all waters and conditions required a near-transparent line, and colour and texture could be added by including a chestnut or a black hair among the white or grey ones. For conditions which required specific colours of line, instructions were available to the angler in Daniel's *Rural Sports* to make his own dye to suit his own purposes. The ingredients might pose something of a challenge to the modern do-it-yourself angler:

Take a pint of strong ale, half a pound of soot, a small quantity of the juice of walnut-leaves, and an equal quantity of alum powdered fine; mix them well, and boil them in a pipkin half an hour; when the mixture is cold, put in the hair, and let it remain for ten or twelve hours.

Some boil a quarter of a pound of soot in a pint of strong alum-water with a little juice of walnut-leaves, for half an hour, and steep the hair in it when nearly cold.

For a *brown*, take some powdered alum, boil it well until dissolved; then add a pound of walnut-tree bark from the branches when the sap is up, or the buds, or green nuts; boil it an hour and let it stand, after skimming it for ten minutes; then put in the *gut* or *hair* for about a minute, (stirring it round,) or until you like the colour. If it continues too long it will become quite dark, and *rot* the hair. The lighter it is tinged with this colour the better. *Salt* and *ale* will also give hair a brownish cast that is steeped in it.

For a *bluish* water colour, proceed as above: only add

A brass line winder used for twisting gut or horsehair lines (casts).

90

logwood instead of walnut, and be careful not to colour it too much.

Yellow; the inner bark of a *crab-tree* boiled in water, with some *alum*, makes a fine yellow, which is excellent when the weeds rot, the line appearing of the same hue. Another may be obtained from two quarts of small ale, and three handfuls of walnut-leaves bruised therein; the hair to remain in it until tinged to your wish.

Tawny is made with lime and water mixed together, by steeping the hair in it for four or five hours, and then soaking it a whole day in a *tan*-pit.

Russet; take a pint of strong *lie* [china tea], half a pint of *soot*, a little juice of walnut-leaves, and a quart of alum water; put them together into a pan, boil them well, and when the liquor is *cold*, steep the hair until it acquires the colour you desire.

A: *Hardy's 'A sportsman's', walking stick seat.* B: *a leather pot-bellied creel with a plain brass latch, by Thompson. Late eighteenth century.* C: *Hardy's 'Unique' salmon fly cabinet, fitted with ten salmon fly trays, with clips to hold 270 flies. The trays were fitted with washable tablets on which to record the flies. There was a space at the bottom to hold Arbo Carbon to keep moths away. Optional extras included trays for sea trout flies, and a solid leather carrying case.* D: *a book of sample flies for trout and salmon fishing, and a selection of gut casts. Also included are a varied collection of hooks to gut. The contents are itemised.* E: *a black and green 'skiver' (leather) tackle wallet with compartments. The central box compartment contains a vellum book which in turn contains looped pages and woollen drying pages.* F: *a fine example of a 1911 model collapsible oak line winder by Hardy's.* G: *Hardy's 1897 model line dryer.* H: *a live bait horn.* I: *a Hardy 'Jock Scott' line winder. This item could be purchased as an optional extra to the reel.* J: *Hardy's 'Curate' combination tool.* K: *a nineteenth century fly tier's hand vice.*

The hair to be dyed should always be the best *white*: the seasons for using dyed hair are September, and two following months for the *yellow*. Russet all the Winter, and until the end of April, as well in rivers as in lakes: for the same periods, the *brown* and *tawny* should be used in brackish, heathy, and moorish Waters.

The various shades in sorrel hairs will naturally furnish lines proper for most waters discoloured by rain, or running on *sand* or *gravel*, particularly when mixed with white; and for bright water, the white alone will be sufficient.

Lines of Silk or Hemp may be coloured by a strong decoction of *Oak bark*, which it is believed resists the water, and adds to their durability: any shade of an excellent *russet brown* may be obtained according to the time they remain in the decoction, which should be used cold.

Hair lines remained virtually unaltered until the end of the nineteenth century, even though silk lines became more widely available from the middle of the century. Keene, writing in his book *Fishing Tackle, its Materials and Manufacture*, published in 1896, still refers to the use of hair lines and favours the hair taken from a young stallion, preferably a thoroughbred and a grey one at that. He also recalls taking hairs from the tail of a famous horse in Hampshire, but as he presumably did not strip the horse bare, this must have been in the nature of a talisman. Keene also comments that some horsehairs are capable of bearing a dead weight of up to two pounds. Although this did not match the weight-bearing capacity of gut, it was quite adequate for fishing smaller fish such as roach on the Thames and was stocked by a majority of the tackle shops up to the turn of the century. Hair lines were suitable for dace and for making up light fly casts and also for use in making the bodies of flies.

Gut lines, made from the gut of silkworm caterpillars, were mostly supplied from Spain. A certain Mr R. Ramsbottom, a gut line manufacturer of 81 Market Street, Manchester, wrote to Keene, who included his account of the business in his book:

Silkworm gut is manufactured chiefly at Murcia, in the south of Spain, situated in a rich and fertile valley abounding in all kinds of fruits. Murcia is an ancient city, formerly a Moorish town, and a considerable number of

The 'Layman Pneumatic Boat', as it appeared in the Fishing Gazette *of 1896. It is interesting to note that this type of craft is again becoming popular in America and is affectionately known as a 'belly boat'.*

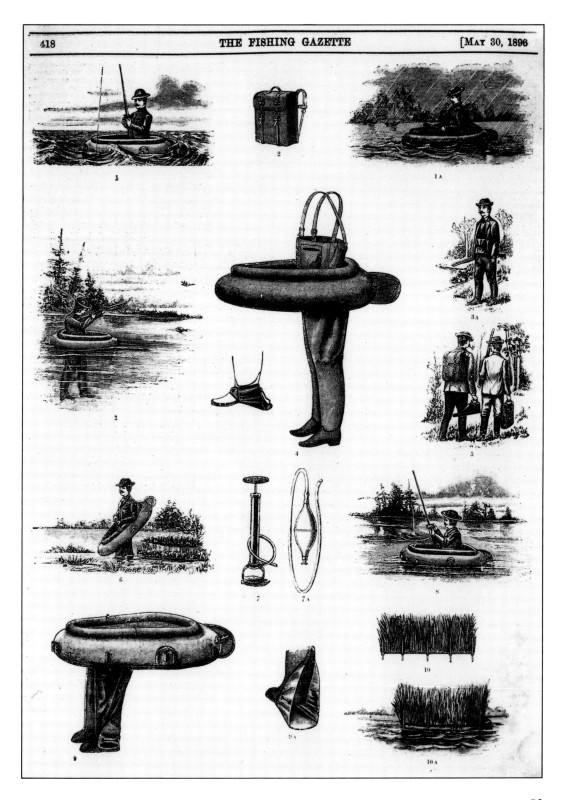

the inhabitants of to-day are descendants of the Moors. For a distance of twelve miles around Murcia the peasants cultivate the silkworm, feeding them on the mulberry leaves, which are most plentiful.

About the beginning of May, the worm is taken and plunged into hot vinegar; and after remaining there for a few hours the workmen slough off the body from the intestine: the latter is then stretched out, and the ends wound round a pin to dry. These threads are then gathered together, (all sizes being mixed), and in a few days they are ready for sale.

The gut is sold in this state by pound weight, and is purchased by the gut manufacturers. The first process to which it is subjected is that of being put into a bath of soap and soda, when the outer skin or scale comes off. It is then laid on rods, and hung up in a room to dry, and thereafter placed in an oven for the purpose of bleaching. After this it

Two early photographs of Allcock's factory in Redditch. At the time they employed nearly one hundred people purely to tie the hooks to the gut (TOP). The hook machine shop (BOTTOM) produced millions of hooks annually for the home and overseas markets.

is given out to girls each of whom, sitting on a low stool, takes a quantity in her lap and puts separately each fibre between the teeth, and rubs it with a wash-leather. Each girl at night, wraps up her work in a clean cloth, to which her number is pinned, and she is paid each night so much per thousand. Next day she takes the same roll of gut and sorts out the various lengths and thicknesses. She then again rubs each strand with wash-leather. After this it is passed to the men, who tie it up in lengths of one hundred each, and wrap the tails with a coarse red thread.

Thus far, the concise and succinct description of a very large manufacturer. I may add, that the silkworm is deemed ready for the process just when it leaves off eating, and a greenish thread is seen protruding from the mouth. Whether or not it would pay to breed the silkworms for the purpose in England, is a matter for other heads than mine. Of course, the gut, when it reaches England, is of a brilliant white pearly hue — just the worst appearance conceivable on a bright clear stream. It is, therefore, stained of a bluish-green or some other colour, according to fancy. Some anglers like a faint green, others a brown, others a yellowish tint, and so on.

The best gut was almost transparent, of good length and as round as possible. While the length of the living caterpillar is about 1½ inches, the optimum length for a salmon line was 10 to 18 inches and for a trout line 13 to 15 inches. The longest gut available in 1885 was 20 inches. The breaking strain of a good quality strand of salmon gut varied from 15 to 18 pounds, which compared very favourably with that of the hair lines.

Ramsbottom's gut traded under the name 'Corta' and prices for the various types and qualities of gut were as follows:

6½in Fine common quality (suitable for making up paternoster traces and hooks for perch, chub, roach and dace)	2d per 100
Medium in same range	4d per 100
8½in Strong in same range	6d per 100
10in Stout in same range	9d per 100
11½in Regular medium strength	1s. per 100
15in Choice gut	4s. per 100
13in Good stout gut for lake fishing	2s 6d per 100
13in Maron or light salmon gut	4s. per 100
11in Refined gut suitable for small flies	1s 6d per 100

While 1 shilling was considered a normal price to pay for a strand or hank of good quality salmon gut in the 1890s, some of extremely fine quality, such as that imported from Spain by Carter and Company, might be as much as 50 shillings.

The *Annual Gut Report* of 1884/5 noted a 6 per cent increase of imports from Spain, raising the total production to 32.5 million pieces of gut, but that the quality was becoming erratic. It was felt that production would improve if British line manufacturers would take a greater interest in the Spanish side of the business where Alcock's had a factory. It was noted that only when British companies introduced their own standards of quality control did things improve noticeably. The Spanish market was further reported to be in

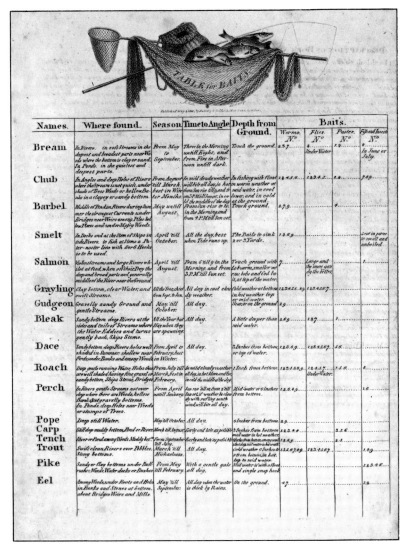

Thess two pages from Daniel's,
Rural Sports give details of the
fish, the baits to use and the times
to fish for them.

some disarray because of a widespread epidemic of cholera.

John Enright & Son of Castle Connell, Ireland, were noted for their gut and casts for salmon and trout. At the Fisheries Exhibition of 1896 they offered 3-yard salmon casts at 9 shillings, and soft twisted salmon casts for heavy fishing, especially in Norway. Their trout casts at 1 shilling were considered not good enough for South of England work, but excellent for Irish lake fishing. A favourite spinning bait on the Shannon was said to be Enright's 'Big Devon', made for them and mounted on extra-strong gut.

The reviewer of the Fisheries Exhibition of 1896 commented on the very competitive price of the gut on the stand of G. Gillett, one of the oldest fishing tackle businesses

DESCRIPTION OF BOBS AND WORMS.

Nº 1 Earth bob, found in sandy or light ground after the Plough the Rooks will direct where this Grub is to be met with by their close attendance upon the plough, is white, bigger than a Gentle with a red head. Another is found in heathy ground with a black or blue head. either of these are to be got by digging one spit deep in the above mentioned Soils, where they have long remained unploughed. Keep them in an earthen vessel well covered with a sufficient quantity of the mould they harbour in, with dryish Mots at top, and let them be in a warm place, are Excellent from beginning of November to middle of April.

Nº 2 Gentles, to be had from putrid Flesh, let them be put into Wheat bran two or three days before used.

Nº 3 Flag Worms, found amongst roots of Flags, is pale yellow, longer and thinner than a Gentle, must be kept like the Cad bait.

Nº 4 Wasp Grubs or Wasp Maggots, are to be in the Cakes of Cells as taken in the nest, before using put them into an Oven, after the bread is drawn, or they may be dried on a Tile before the fire just to harden and make them tough.

Nº 5 Cowdung bob or Clap bait, found under a Cow drop from May till Michaelmas, is larger but like a Gentle, in its native Earth as Nº 1 is to be preserved.

Nº 6 Cadis Worm or Cad bait, found under loose stones in shallow rivers or brooks, are covered with Husks of Sticks, Straw, Rushes and Stones, they are yellow bigger than a Gentle with a black or blue head. Keep them in flannel or linen bags, and dip them bag and all into Water once a day for five or six days, they will then become tough and fitter for angling, than when first taken from the water.

Nº 7 Lob or Dew Worm, found in Gardens, is very large having a red head a streak down the back and a broad flat Tail. those with a Knot are fit only for Eels.

Nº 8 Marsh Worm, found in marshy ground are of a blueish colour, and require more scouring in Mots than most other worms, are a good bait from March to Michaelmas.

Nº 9 Brandling Red or Blood Worm, found in rotten Dunghills and Tanners Bark that has been used. The red worm found at the root of a great Dock, and which lies wrapt up in a round clew is a particular bait for Bream. The common red worm is very good for all small fish.

FLIES WHERE FOUND.

Nº 1 Stone Fly, under hollow stones at the sides of Rivers, is of a brown colour with yellow streaks on the back and belly, has large wings. In Season from April to July.

Nº 2 Green Drake, among stones by Rivers side, has a yellow body ribbed with green, is long and slender, his wings like a Butter Flies, his tail turns on his back. Very good from May to Midsummer.

Nº 3 Oak Fly, upon the body of an old Oak or Ash tree with its head downwards, is of a brown colour from May to September. Excellent for Trout in a clear water, putting a Cad bait on the point of the hook, and letting it sink a few inches and gradually raising it.

Nº 4 Palmer Fly or Worm, upon the leaves of plants, is commonly called a Caterpillar, when it turns to a Fly, very good for Trout.

Nº 5 Ant Fly, in Ant hills from June to September, a handfull of the Earth, with as much of the grass that grews on their hillocks put into a glass bottle with the Ant flies, will keep them alive.

Nº 6 May Fly, playing at the River side especially before Rain.

Nº 7 Black Fly, upon every Hawthorn after the buds appear. Mem: Artificial Flies may be procured at the shops where fishing Tackle is sold. Worms of various sorts, and other baits, are also generally kept in the season, ready prepared for use.

PASTES, HOW TO BE MADE.

Nº 1 Red Paste, the crumb of fine new white bread without being made wet, worked up in the hand and coloured with Vermilion, as near as possible to that of the Salmons Row.

Nº 2 Brown Paste, the crumb of brown bread mixed with honey, worked up in the same manner.

Nº 3 Blood of a Sheeps heart mixed with honey and flour, and worked to a proper consistency.

Nº 4 Old Cheese grated Butter, sufficient to work it, and coloured with Saffron. If in Winter use the fat of roasty bacon instead of butter.

Nº 5 Crumbs of bread worked with honey or sugar, moistened with Gum Ivy water.

Nº 6 Bread chewed and worked in the hand untill stiff.

FISH AND INSECTS.

Nº 1 Minnow.	Nº 6 Yellow Frog.
2 Gudgeon.	7 Snail slit.
3 Roach.	8 Grasshopper.
4 Dace.	9 Beetle.
5 Smelt.	10 Shrimp.

in London, and went on to relate the possibly apocryphal story of the late Mr Gillett's passion for Spanish gut. Having at last been forced to abandon hair, Mr Gillett bought as much quality gut as he could lay his hands on when he considered the price to be advantageous, and stored it by having his chairs, sofas and beds stuffed with it. The writer wryly commented, 'when one comes to think of it, gut seems more natural inside than hair.'

Drawn gut was a cheap alternative to the naturally tapered gut. The gut was trimmed by drawing it through a steel plate, perforated with a series of graduated holes until the desired degree of taper was achieved, since the gut was literally shaved by the steel. The process tended to weaken the gut and it could cause fraying.

Gimp was a fine, unwoven silk line bound with spaced coils of brass wire and was mainly used for traces for pike fishing. The line was treated in several ways to tone down and discolour the brass wire to prevent it glinting in the water. The substances commonly used were a solution of chloride of platinum or a weak solution of nitric acid, but these had the disadvantage of weakening the silk line, and a better method was to use black lead fixed with a varnish.

Towards the end of the nineteenth century it was generally regarded as cheaper to buy running lines and fly lines ready-made. The main centres of production were Manchester, Redditch and Nottingham. Companies such as Walter Wells and Martin's of Newark-on-Trent produced high-quality lines. Martin's were especially noted for an 8-ply plaited silk line, sold undressed at 3s 4d per yard. In the 1890s Carter & Company sold 40-yard double-tapered salmon lines for 10s 6d and 100-yard plaited silk pike lines at 6 shillings.

Raw silk lines were imported from America. These were made from unboiled silk and were popular because they were both cheap and durable. They were available both dressed and undressed — the former at a higher price. Anglers were encouraged to apply their own dressings and several recipes were published. Dr Emil Weeger, first president of the Moravian Piscatorial Society, recommended a mixture of pure resin and solid paraffin to keep the line flexible. Extra solid paraffin was to be added in winter to compensate for the tendency of the cold water to stiffen the line which made it more difficult to handle. Coloured paint could be added to the dressing to tint the line to an appropriate shade.

Line dryers, or winders, were developed towards the end of the nineteenth century to dry the new silk line quickly because it would rot if it was allowed to remain damp. They were also useful for changing and storing line. Most were of a folding wood and metal frame construction. Hardy's 'Bethune' line winder first appeared in the 1908 catalogue. The reel could be attached to the handle of the winder which had fittings corresponding to the butt end of the rod. The line could then be wound evenly on to the frame by means of an oscillating guide. Made in two sizes for salmon and trout lines, the winders were packed in cedar boxes. Some could be attached to tables. Some, like the 1911 model, were made all of brass on an oak stand, and a small, folding and portable version was available.

LANDING NETS

The design of landing nets has remained largely unchanged for a very long time. Early nets were often home-made, the net being attached to a hoop of iron, whalebone or bent

An interior view of the 'Sussex Piscatorial Society's club room at 142 Kings-road Arches, Brighton.

ashwood on the end of a long wood pole. By the end of the eighteenth century the refinement of a hoop detachable, by means of a brass or iron threaded ferrule, was available. Another innovation that rendered the landing net more portable was the hinged iron hoop, which folded to half its size. Fly fishermen commonly used the landing net for fish of 4 to 6 pounds, beyond which a gaffe would be necessary. Now much larger fish are netted in landing nets which have not altered materially since the turn of the century.

A classic net and one which combined nearly all of the innovations was the Hardy's Improved Y-Shaped Collapsing Landing Net which is illustrated in the 1888 catalogue and cost 25 shillings. Cholmondeley-Pennell refers both to this net

From the Hardy catalogue of 1888, which not only included rods and reels, but also a wide variety of angling accessories.

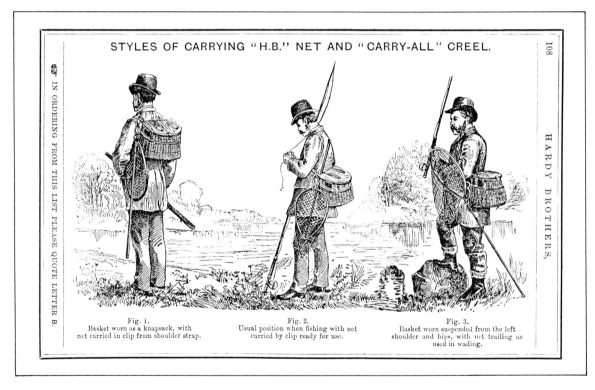

STYLES OF CARRYING "H.B." NET AND "CARRY-ALL" CREEL.

108

IN ORDERING FROM THIS LIST PLEASE QUOTE LETTER B.

HARDY BROTHERS,

Fig. 1.
Basket worn as a knapsack, with net carried in clip from shoulder strap.

Fig. 2.
Usual position when fishing with net carried by clip ready for use.

Fig. 3.
Basket worn suspended from the left shoulder and hips, with net trailing as used in wading.

and to another, recently on the market, by Williams of Great Queen Street. Williams's net first developed the telescopic handle, and a carrying strap attached to the handle enabled the angler to hold the net at his side and, at the jerk of his wrist, to extend the net and unfold the Y-shaped fitting that formed the triangular net. At a fisheries exhibition in 1896 Hardy Brothers showed an enormous landing net with an 8 foot hickory handle and a net of 2½ feet diameter, a copy of a net made for a client, Sir Waldie Griffiths. A reviewer of the exhibition makes the comment: 'there is no doubt that the use of such a net would save the lives of hundreds of Kelts as well as prove most useful in landing clean fish from a high bank or other difficult place.'

Others available at the end of the century included the Pocket Landing Net, which simply had a short handle and a fixed hoop net that was easy to carry. Farlow's also produced an Improved Landing Net, with a solid hoop but with a handle that folded in half. The net itself was generally made of fine cord or waterproofed silk. Some rod-tip tubes were fitted with a threaded ferrule to which could be attached a net head or gaff, or they could be used as a wading staff.

GAFFS

The basic gaff was an iron hook attached to an ash or bamboo pole, which was used mainly for salmon fishing to assist in landing a fish too large to be handled with the landing net. While the hook was the usual form of terminal, an alternative was a straight spike or barbed spear which did not curve away from the handle. The handles varied in length and were usually either ash, stained and varnished, or bamboo.

Bamboo gaff handles suffered from one serious design fault, the connecting ferrule was invariably not cross-pinned to the bamboo pole but merely wedged or slotted on to it. The result was that the head was inclined to twist and loosen. How many gaffs now lie at the bottom of river beds, having fallen in or been hurled there in countless fits of rage and frustration? The redoubtable H. Cholmondeley-Pennell was clearly not willing to put up with this unsatisfactory state of affairs. Characteristic of a man who had redesigned the reel, incorporating all the best features then available, he had Farlows make him a gaff with the head fixed by means of a steel rivet. This passed through not only the brass ferrule but the bamboo pole and the screw of the head, thus locking all the parts together.

The handle of the gaff was sometimes hollowed out, or the natural hollow of the bamboo could be used, as a container for alternative tips for the rod. Pocket-sized gaffs, which simply had short handles, were also available for easy carrying. Another device which attempted to cut down on the endless impedimenta an angler was obliged to carry was a combined gaff/priest — a gaff with a short handle, about 12 inches long, with a heavy brass or lead terminal.

The most desirable gaffs for the collector are undoubtedly the fine examples, made throughout the nineteenth century, with handles either of telescopic brass or well-turned wood. These are often fitted with a plated steel head and a ring at the end of the handle by the attachment of a lanyard, this can be used both for carrying and for retaining the gaff. Named examples are especially desirable and the maker's stamp can often be found on the protective flap or shield of the head.

Gaffs have, for many years, been frowned upon and often forbidden in some areas — especially at certain times of the season — because of the damage they cause to fish. If, when a fish has been landed by this means, it is found not to be in peak condition, and this applies particularly to salmon, it cannot be returned but has to be dispatched.

PRIESTS

The derivation of this term is uncertain, so it has still to be assumed that it was coined by a cynic who saw it as administering the last rites. The priest is used to dispatch a landed fish and takes the form of a small cudgel — a short tapered handle with a bulbous head. The priest might be in one piece or in two, with a head weighted with lead, size and weight depended on the size of fish for which it was intended.

Many anglers were content to use whatever came to hand — a stick or a stone — or to fashion their own, for the priest was usually considered as purely functional and of little

A painting by A. Roland Knight entitled A pike coming to the gaff, *c.1900, (oil on canvas, 14 × 22 in.*

consequence. However, occasional specimens can be found, probably made for presentation, which are of bone or ebony with silver mounts. Towards the end of the nineteenth century tackle manufacturers began to exploit the growing market and included priests in their range of equipment. Hardy's priest, of turned wood with neat bulbous head and bearing the maker's name, is a good example of the type. It first appeared in their catalogue in the 1920s and remained in production until the 1939-45 war.

FLOATS

Floats are of such an ephemeral nature that few early examples have survived for the collector. Those that can now be found almost invariably come from no earlier than the turn of this century and, since types and techniques have remained constant throughout the period, dating specimens is far from easy.

In some respects the float is to the coarse fisherman what the fly is to the fly fisherman. Floats are made in a wide variety of types and patterns to cater for both fish and water. There are floats for fast-flowing water, slow-flowing water, lakes and sea angling. Anglers have become accustomed to being able to buy whatever they need and manufacturers have been keen to provide ranges of equipment which leave little

A: *a nineteenth-century trout trophy mounted on oak;* B: *a twentieth-century zinc bait can;* C: *a leather fly book presented to a Mr Harrison in 1840, for taking the heaviest 'jack' on the Thames;* D: *a wooden creel, with hinged lid and oval fish hatch, c.1800;* E: *a nineteenth-century turned wooden priest;* F: *a Victorian hand-held version of a gut twisting engine;* G: *an ivory and treen fisherman's compendium from the nineteenth century;* H: *turned wooden fly boxes;* I: *a jointed brass clearing ring (this type was still being supplied by Carter & Co. Ltd in 1933, in its original form).*

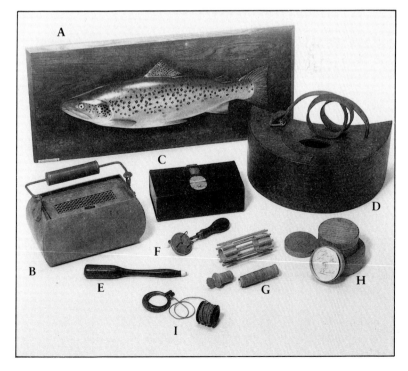

scope for individual invention. Prior to the expansion of the tackle industry a century ago, however, much was left to be made by the individual angler and many publications were available to offer advice on techniques and materials.

Daniel's *Rural Sports* describes how a float should be made:

Floats are of many kinds; of Swan, Goose, and Muscovy Duck and Porcupine quills; the first is preferable when *light* baits are used in rivers or deep waters, the others are for slow streams or ponds, where the water is not very deep, and where the baits are pastes, etc. The quills of the *bustard* some anglers use, believing that the small black spots with which they are said to be mottled, appear to the fish as so many little flies, and attract them by this deception. For heavy fishing with worm or minnow, and in rapid eddies, the Cork float is best, and is made by taking a cork free from flaws, and with a small red-hot iron bore a hole lengthways through the centre; it is then to be cut across the grain with a sharp knife, about two-thirds of the length, and the remaining third (which is the top of the float) rounded with it, and then neatly finished with pumice stone; the whole resembling in shape a child's peg top: for *Pike, Barbel*, and large *Chub*, the cork should be the size of a small Bergamot pear; for *Trout, Perch* and *Eels*, not bigger than a walnut when the green rind is removed; a quill is fitted to the hole, and used *formerly* to be cut off close to the cork at each end of it. Some direct cork floats to be proportioned to the number of hairs the line is made of, and no larger than a *horse-bean* for a single hair; but so diminutive a cork is of no use, and the Quill floats will answer better. Some recommend the shape of a cork like a pear, and not to exceed the size of a nutmeg, and the quill that passes through it not to be more than half an inch above and below the cork; they are now made with a cap at the top, and wire for the line to pass through at the bottom. The advantage the *cork* float has over the *bare quill* is, that it allows the line to be leaded so *heavily* that the hook sinks almost as soon as put in the water; whereas *lightly* leaded, it does not reach the bottom until near the end of the swim. In leading of lines great care is needful to balance the floats so *nicely* that a very small touch will sink them. Some use, for this purpose, lead shaped like a barley-corn, but shot are better; and for fine fishing have a number of *small* in preference to a few *large* shot on the line; the lowest of either ought to be nine or ten inches from the hook.

IX *A small part of the Marchant Lane collection.*

X. A collection of antique accessories, including gaffs, floats and lures

The cork float was the most robust of all, but was not suitable when great accuracy was required. Then a much finer and thinner float was required, made of a single quill only and needing very little lead weight to make it stand in the water. Daniel goes on to give advice on how the quill float is to be made:

> Quill floats are thus made: the barrel part is cut off from that where the feathers grow, the inside cleared from the film, and a small piece of pitch fixed close to the end; a piece of cotton is then introduced, and upon that another piece of pitch, which not only confines the cotton, but assists in making the float discernible in water. A piece of soft wood, the size of the quill, about two inches long, of which nearly one inch is to be introduced into the quill, after being dipped into a melted Cement of bees-wax, rosin and chalk, in equal quantities; the lower end of this plug is to be tapered, with a fine awl and a piece of brass twisted wire, with a round eye at the end, is to be passed as a screw into the plug, with a pair of pliers, turning the float round; the line passes through this eye of the wire, and the upper part of the quill is fastened to the line by a hoop made of a larger size quill, so as to admit the thickness of the line, and which ought to fasten nearly an inch from the top of the quill. (These *caps* should be secured by fine waxed silk, varnished over, which prevents their splitting; and so also should the end of the quill round the plug; which will

A: *an ivory tackle compendium. The frame is composed of ten line spokes, the centre unscrews, and itself, provides four separate compartments for items such as shot, float caps, wax and silk. Included are two intricate bobbins, each with silk supply. The whole is contained in a card case with a screw top. This example dates from the late 1700s. They are more commonly found in treen (wood) dating from the early 1800s.* **B:** *a late nineteenth-century walking stick rod. The whole rod could be stored in the butt section which had a silver-plated screw cap, engraved 'W. Osborn, maker, 26 North Street, Exeter'. The rod comprises: whole cane butt, greenheart middle sections and split-cane tip.* **C:** *a Victorian three-section telescopic brass gaff with hook guard. The hand of this example is made of lignum vitae. Makers names, if applied, are generally found on the hook guard.* **D:** *a Staffordshire pottery meat plate, printed in blue with an angling scene. On the reverse is a printed mark 'British Scenery', c.1830.*

greatly preserve the float.) These hoops, and the top of the floats, may be dyed red, (which will render them more conspicuous,) by putting as much powdered Brazil wood into stale chamber-lie as will make it a deep red, which may be seen by applying it upon a piece of white paper; then take some spring water, and put a handful of salt, and a small quantity of *Argol* into it; stir them until they are dissolved, and boil them well in a saucepan; when the water is *cold* scrape the quills, and steep them a little time in the mixture; afterwards let them remain in the chamber-lie for a fortnight, and, after drying, rub them with a woollen cloth, and they will be transparent.

If two quills are wanted to be joined together, it may be done by a plug a little thicker in the middle than at the ends, which are to go into the mouths of the quills; dip the two ends in the above cement warmed, and fix the quills upon it, or by dipping the ends of both quills, *without the plug*, into the cement, and inserting one into the other while thoroughly warm, the cement when cold will strongly fix them; rub the float all over with wet coal dust and woollen cloth, dry it with one of linen, and after that dry coal dust will polish it effectually. Quill floats should be so leaded as to just suffer their tops to appear above the surface, that the slightest nibble may be perceived; if either a cork or quill-float fall on *one side*, the lead is either on the ground or insufficient to keep them in a proper position.

An 'English wicker fishing basket' (TOP LEFT) and the 'Expanding Salmon bag' (BOTTOM LEFT) were both marketed by Hardy's in the late 1880s. Creels were often made of leather, like this late eighteenth century 'pot-bellied' example (BELOW).

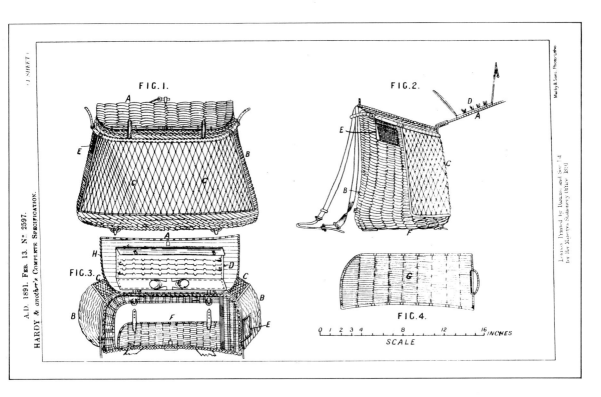

The original drawings for the Hardy 'Perfect creel', patented in 1891.

Daniel goes on to suggest that the line should be a foot shorter than the rod, which implies that a reel was not used in this form of fishing. This equipment appears more in the nature of a roach pole which was fished without a reel. It is also recommended that a 14- or 15-foot rod be used, which should be light but with a stiff top, the extremity to be made of whalebone.

Keene, writing almost 80 years later, differs remarkably little in his description of floats. He does, however, refer to seeing float production at Alcock's factory at Redditch, which was turning out thousands a week but still scarcely able to meet the insatiable demand. Alcock's was one only of a number of factories producing similar floats, and it is remarkable that out of the prodigious quantities made, so few should have survived. Although the sport of angling was growing rapidly in popularity at this time, it seems unlikely that anglers of a century ago were either so careless with their floats, or so numerous, as to require so great a number. Perhaps the situation was something akin to that of the fly fisherman, who likes to have a greater variety of size and type of fly than is really necessary to attract the fish. It would appear that the manufacturers were at least as adept at catching the angler as the angler was at catching the fish.

STEPHEN ELMER: Still life with pike, carp, roach, perch, brown trout and a creel. *Oil on canvas, 25 × 29 in., painted c.1780. Elmer was amongst the first artists to paint still life studies of fish.*

J. R. Richardson, in the late nineteenth century, offered the Kingston Bite Indicator. 'A little affair for slipping on to the top of your float of an evening, to enable you to see it better'. A contemporary commented that a bit of white feather would do just as well.

CREELS
A creel is a basket for carrying the catch. The earliest surviving creels are made of leather and the Fly Fisher's Club in London possesses the one reputedly owned by Izaac Walton in the seventeenth century, which is of typical pot-bellied form. A cheaper and lighter form was made of wicker and it is these that are most often seen in angling pictures of the nineteenth century. Wood creels of the eighteenth and early nineteenth century were crescent-shaped to fit the waist. A popular form of creel in the latter part of the nineteenth century was made of plywood, which was strong and light and had the added advantage of forming a seat for the angler. Also in this period, bags were made of waterproof materials, but the Ogden & Scotford Fishing Bag of 1896 included a new feature — a washable, detachable, waterproof fish-holding division, which had large brass eyelet holes all over it to allow air to get to the fish. At about the same time, J.R. Richardson marketed a similar bag in three sizes, named the Surbition Bag.

CHAPTER SIX

Hardy's of Alnwick

Two Hardy 'Perfect' fly reels, showing the difference between the 1891 patent 2½ in. (LEFT) and the 1896 patent 2½ in. (RIGHT), with the two-piece frame connected by nickel pillars. The 'Perfect' reel developed rapidly between these two dates, giving rise to a number of variants. At the Fisheries Exhibition in March 1895 a new reel was noticed on the Hardy stand and an extract from the Fishing Gazette read:

'The framework has been made in one solid piece without joints. It is claimed for it that it has a specially contrived regulator which admits the possibility of the fish striking itself; does away with the requirement that the Angler should hold the line, and. is easy of Regulation with either hand.'

In 1872 William Hardy established his business in Paikes Street, Alnwick, Northumberland. He was the eldest son of John James Hardy, the County Coroner for North Northumberland, who came from an old Redesdale family. The Hardy family as a whole had for long been keen sportsmen and it had only been a question of time before they had become involved with angling as well as shooting. At first, however, the Hardys were gunsmiths and metal workers or cutlers.

The manufacture of sporting guns was by that time well established and dominated by the famous London companies. There was little room left in the market for an unknown provincial maker, and the scope of Hardy's gunmaking activity was confined to the local area and was not to expand. The fishing tackle industry, however, was in a very different position. The sport was growing in popularity at a great rate and the manufacture of tackle was developing from the limitations of a cottage industry to a basis of mass production in a small number of centres. While there existed many companies producing tackle of all kinds to cater for the

111

increased demand, none was producing goods of the standard common in the production of sporting guns. Hardy's were to change all that, and in a very short space of time.

William Hardy was soon joined in the business by his second brother John James (junior), who saw the potential of the tackle market and was largely instrumental in steering the business away from gunmaking. He remained for many years the innovative, driving force in the company.

Hardy's are now known for their range of reels as much as for any aspect of tackle manufacture, but this was not where the emphasis was first applied. In the first years of its existence the firm concentrated mainly on rod building and especially on the construction of the split-cane rod. The manufacture of three- and four-strip cane rods had been established in Britain by about 1800, but towards the middle of the nineteenth century American makers had developed the six-strip rod. These superior rods soon dominated the British market and were widely copied by the British rod makers. J. J. Hardy determined to challenge the supremacy of the American manufacturers.

By the 1800s Hardy's had a good selection of top-quality cane rods in production. That decade saw them carry off many awards and medals at angling exhibitions for their development of the split-cane rod in all its forms — for salmon and trout fishing. The Great Fisheries Exhibition of 1883/4 in London gave them the opportunity to show the world just what they could do in rod making. They seized that opportunity, and records show that they returned with hundreds of pounds worth of orders and an international reputation.

Generations of Hardys, having all been expert anglers, knew by personal experience what was required of a rod. J. J. Hardy himself was a champion of international casting events. It is recorded that at one of the annual fishing exhibitions at the Royal Aquarium he gave a demonstration of the power of their hexagonal split bamboo rods by landing a strong swimmer from the swimming bath.

Success in business, both in arriving at the top and maintaining that position, customarily depends on pioneering new ideas. Hardy's have certainly been responsible for a steady stream of significant inventions. As early as 1882 the 'lockfast joint' was patented and in 1890 bridge rings were invented and gradually began to replace snake rings. In 1894 joints of rods were further improved by the addition of splint ends. At the Fisheries Exhibition of 1900 Hardy's introduced the nonagonal salmon rod which received enthusiastic reviews in the influential *Fishing Gazette*. Invention continued with two significant developments in 1911. These were the screw-grip reel fitting and the C.C. de France rod, the 7-foot version of which at 2¾ ounces was the world's lightest rod. With such a series of successful inventions their reputation quickly spread and they were recognized as the leading rod builder in Britain. It also provided strong competition with the leading American manufacturers, such as Charles Orvis of Vermont and Hiram Leonard of Central Valley, near New York, who were already famous for rod building. British anglers, no doubt in the spirit of patriotism then running high, were keen to patronise the British company. There was no other manufacturer to match them for quality on the home ground.

Left to right: Mr D. Hardy, Mr J. Hardy and Mr Wm. F. Hardy examining some of the rods made at their factory in Alnwick.

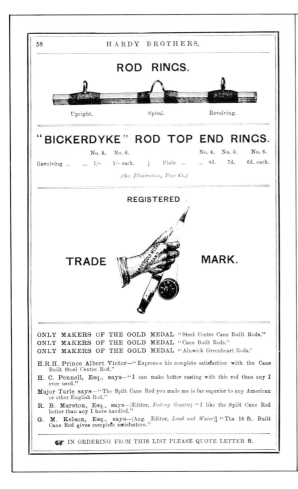

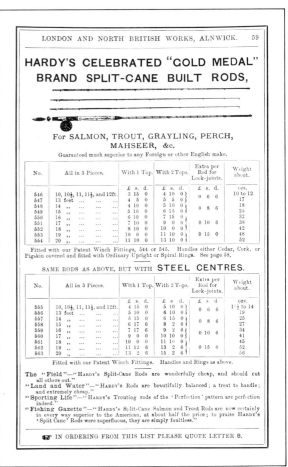

Indeed, quality control was one of the key ingredients of the company's rapid rise and its ability to maintain its position. Mr Henry Clark, a retired employee of Hardy's, who was trained at the Alnwick factory during the 1930s recalls the standards set by Mr L.R.H. Hardy at a time when the workers were remunerated on a piece rate. It was Hardy's custom to visit the workshops during the lunch period carrying a club hammer. Any work he found which failed to meet his exacting requirements was instantly destroyed - not only the offending piece, but the entire batch from which it came.

World domination of the market may have been achieved through autocratic management, but it was also a management which would go to any lengths to satisfy the customer. Hardy's were proud to number among their customers not only the cream of society — Prince Albert Victor (Duke of Clarence), the King of Belgium and the

In the early 1880s Hardy's produced their first steel-centred rods and from then on it became an option on their range of split-cane rods.

Emperor of Germany — but also the acknowledged leaders of the angling fraternity — H. Cholmondeley-Pennell, W. Senior, editor of *The Field*, and R.B. Marston, editor of *Fishing Gazette*. Later, Queen Mary was to turn to Hardy's to commission a miniature rod for the celebrated doll's house at Windsor, a rod which is perfect in all its working detail. In the brief space of 15 years Hardy's had raised the standard of rod making to the same levels reached by the leading gun makers and had attracted customers from all over the world.

Testimonials from influential customers were put to good use and were often published in the company's catalogues:

MARLBOROUGH HOUSE, PALL MALL, S.W.

Capt. Greville is desired by Prince Albert Victor to express his complete satisfaction with the steel centre cane-built rod which was recently supplied by Messrs Hardy Brothers.

The following testimonial from George Kelson, a noted angling writer, appeared in the 1888 catalogue:

Sirs

I beg to inform you that I gave the rod (what became known as the Kelson Salmon Rod) a good trial whilst I was in the north fishing in the rivers Tay and Lyon. The whole time I was there the weather was extremely rough and boisterous. The 'ill wind' however, will blow you no harm, for after working the rod for several days, to my complete satisfaction it showed no sign of distress whatever. I mention this particularly, as you are aware that I use a very long line when it is necessary, and nothing tries a rod more than making a 'wind cast' with it. I hate paying compliments, but in justice to yourselves I candidly admit that you have admirably succeeded in following my instructions, and getting the required action for making all the various salmon cast. So satisfied am I that I intend not only to recommend the rod, but always to use it myself.

I am faithfully yours,
George Kelson 13 May 1887

HYDE PARK CORNER, S.W. *18 February 1885*

Dear Sirs

You ask my report as to the Split-Cane Trout Rod you built for me last spring. I have given away three out of my four other trout rods, keeping one only as a stand by, for I now care to use no other than your little cane wonder.

I have used it hard this past season on all kinds of trout, including sea trout, and say it is perfect in action, balance, and power, except in one branch of fishing, that is 'dry fly', with gossamer gut on large fish, in which it is rather *too stiff.*

The screw point I swear *by*, and not *at*; and the winch and its fitting are simple, yet effective. The cork handle is the best I have ever had hold of, especially when fishing in wet weather or cold winds.

Judging from the killing powers of this little 10ft rod on heavy fighting trout, I think it the most effective trout rod I have yet handled; it has not even yet cracked its varnish, though it has seen hard work in plenty.

Truly yours
W. Baden-Powell

Testimonials flowed in from all parts of the world and the following are typical examples:

Dear Sirs

I am sending you to be thoroughly overhauled the two split-cane rods you built for me three years ago, viz the 12ft Split Cane (plain) and the 14ft Split Cane (steel centred). As you will be able to see for yourselves, both

OPPOSITE: *The original patent drawings for the 'Perfect' fly reel granted in January 1891.*

From the Hardy Brothers catalogue of 1888.

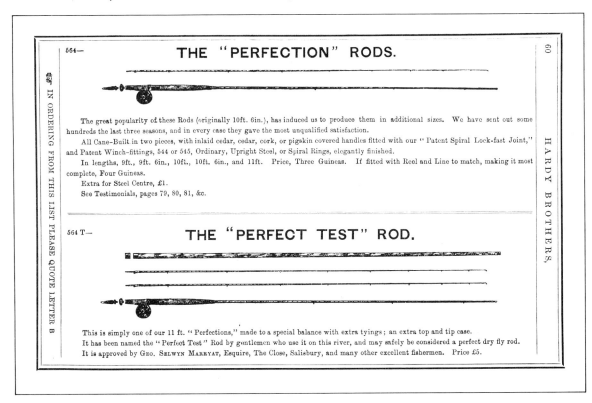

564—

THE "PERFECTION" RODS.

The great popularity of these Rods (originally 10ft. 6in.), has induced us to produce them in additional sizes. We have sent out some hundreds the last three seasons, and in every case they gave the most unqualified satisfaction.

All Cane-Built in two pieces, with inlaid cedar, cedar, cork, or pigskin covered handles fitted with our "Patent Spiral Lock-fast Joint," and Patent Winch-fittings, 544 or 545, Ordinary, Upright Steel, or Spiral Rings, elegantly finished.

In lengths, 9ft., 9ft. 6in., 10ft., 10ft. 6in., and 11ft. Price, Three Guineas. If fitted with Reel and Line to match, making it most complete, Four Guineas.

Extra for Steel Centre, £1.

See Testimonials, pages 79, 80, 81, &c.

564 T—

THE "PERFECT TEST" ROD.

This is simply one of our 11 ft. "Perfections," made to a special balance with extra tyings; an extra top and tip case.

It has been named the "Perfect Test" Rod by gentlemen who use it on this river, and may safely be considered a perfect dry fly rod.

It is approved by GEO. SELWYN MARRYAT, Esquire, The Close, Salisbury, and many other excellent fishermen. Price £5.

IN ORDERING FROM THIS LIST PLEASE QUOTE LETTER B

HARDY BROTHERS,

69

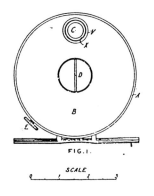

FIG.1.

SCALE

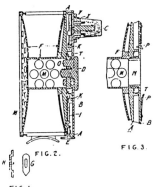

FIG.2.

FIG.3.

FIG.4.

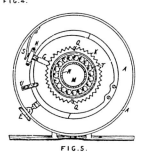

FIG.5.

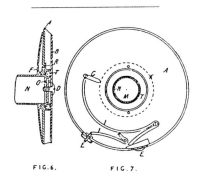

FIG.6.   FIG.7.

rods have seen a great deal of work and the more I use them the more I like them. Instead of trying the 14ft rod on Mahseer as I had intended, I changed my plans and started on a trip to East Central Africa. I fished in the upper waters of the Wahmi a good deal for Siluroid with this rod and the strain I put on it on one occasion to hold a 31lb. Silurus in rapid water from getting into the branches of a fallen tree lying across the river was almost more than I could hold. The bank was very sloping and I do not exaggerate when I say that several times the tip and butt were not more than 3ft apart. I every moment expected a general smash, but gimp, trace and heavy line ably seconded the strain on your rod, and after he was banked the rod went out as straight as when it left your hands. I cannot sufficiently praise it . . .

Yours faithfully
George H. Johnston, late 12th Royal Lancers, 1886

Dear Sirs

I have been using your split-cane rod sent out last season, and it is a little 'gem', and although virtually a fly rod I use it at times for spinning, without doing it the slightest damage. I would not care to go back to the greenheart.

Yours truly
Robert Ticehurst
Christchurch, New Zealand, 14 Dec. 1887

No doubt Hardy's international reputation was greatly assisted by the influence of the British Empire, then reaching its zenith. The testimonials and the company's records attest to the fact that both British and foreign anglers put in their special requests for equipment to suit conditions in India, Australia, New Zealand, Canada, America, Africa and the Far East. Special rods and tracers were made for fishing mahseer in India. In 1931 five Rhodesian Reels were commissioned, all of one size and probably an adaptation of an existing model, modified to suit local conditions, perhaps for tiger fishing. In 1934 the South African Surf Casting Reel was developed for fishing off the South African coast as was also the Natal Surf Reel. Several rods were named after lakes in New Zealand and a special gaff was included in an exhibition in 1896 which took the form of a miniature salmon gaff, designed for the large trout found in New Zealand water. A commentary on the exhibition described the gaff:

Early in 1931, using Hardy tackle, Zane Grey landed the first ever Great Tahitian Striped Marlin.

Hardy Brothers' New Zealand customers asked them to see if they could send out a gaff to carry in a sling for landing big trout, and therefore much smaller than that used in this country for salmon and pike. They showed us what they had made, viz., a very perfect gaff for large trout; it is carried slung from the shoulder, like a Hampshire dry fly net. The point is protected and the gaff retained in position by an ingenious and very simple little metal loop.

The cover of the 1888 edition of the *Angler's Guide and Sporting Catalogue* proudly declared that 27 prize medals and diplomas had been obtained since 1881. At the Fisheries Exhibition in London in 1883 Hardy's were awarded the gold medal for the best trout rod as well as £10 for the best collection of trout rods, against an entry from 52 other competitors. *The Field*, in its edition of 27th June 1885, included a press notice from a recent inventions exhibition which described some interesting developments in rod making, showing to what extent Hardy's had then broken into the American market by producing a double-built cane rod. The rod was composed of 12 sections of cane, six within six, so that the core was formed not of the soft inner part but of the hard skin or enamel of the outside, so giving much greater strength and power. A further improvement was noted in the introduction of a steel inner core which was tapered in proportion to the thickness of the rod. The steel was hardened by tempering and did not add unduly to the weight, merely a few ounces for a salmon rod, but gave it immense casting power and helped prevent warping. On the same stand was shown the Universal reel fitting, a W-shaped fitting which had been invented by Hardy's in 1873. The company was the only one at that exhibition to be awarded a prize medal for rods and tackle.

A report of the Yachting Exhibition in 1896 eulogized the Hardy display. The report also illustrated a style of business promotion which was obviously successful. The rods designed for famous individuals were put into commercial production and bore the prestigious name as a mark of confidence.

This celebrated Alnwick firm, ever moving in the paths of progress, is again exhibiting at the Yachting Exhibition at the Royal Aquarium, Westminster, and will remain over the 'Fisheries' which follows. The novelties to be inspected at Messrs. Hardy's stall are well-nigh endless and, of

A: *the 4½ in. 'Perfect' reel by Hardy's.* **B:** *probably the most famous of the Hardy big game reels, the 'Zane Grey'. This is a 4³⁄₁₆ in. model which retailed for £25 in 1937. Constructed of Monel metal it was guaranteed to be absolutely immune to the action of sea water and air in any part of the world. It was a requirement of Mr Zane Grey that if it carried his name it should be the best reel in the world.*

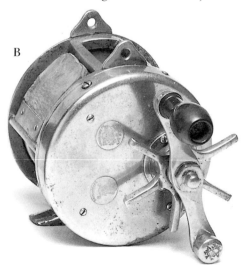

A   B

course, the standard goods which have made the firm famous all over the world are to be seen and handled. In cane-built steel centre salmon rods, half a dozen renowned patterns are on view. These are:

1. The KELSON, 18ft. double cane-built as made for G.H. Kelson Esq., without steel centre: £10/15s.; with steel centre: £12/5s.

2. The CHAMPION, 17ft.6ins. double cane-built, as used by Mr John Hardy in his champion and record cast at the late Scarborough Exhibition. By the way, this is not a rod built for tournament purposes, but a legitimate fishing rod, and the price: £12/5s.

3. The SPECIAL salmon rod recommended is 17ft. double cane-built, steel centre, as used by the editor of *The Field*, a most useful all-round rod, price: £11/6s.

4. The celebrated HI REGAN, 16ft. double cane-built, steel centre as made for the editor of the work *How and where to fish in Ireland*, is a powerful salmon rod with clean, easy action, and the price: £10/-.

5.Is a beautiful type of ladies salmon rod, 14ft. double cane-built, steel centre: £7/3/6d.; 15ft.: £8/11s.; and 15ft.6ins. : £9/13s.

6.The PENNELL, double cane-built with steel centre as made for and used by H. Cholmondeley-Pennell Esq: £9/5s.

In cane built trout rods equal excellence is apparent, and naturally a more numerous selection, owing to the different lengths and weights to suit the tastes and fancies of individual anglers. The special HOUGHTON is a dry fly rod, 10-11ft.: £5/5s.; the PERFECTION, in two pieces: £3/3s.; the MARSTON PERFECTION, as used by R.B. Marston, editor of the *Fishing Gazette*: £3/3s.; the ALBERT VICTOR, as made for H.R.H. the late Prince Albert Victor, 10ft.6ins. steel centre: £5/16/6d.; the PRINCESS as made for H.R.H. Princess May, 9ft. to 10 ft. steel centre: £7/7s.; the PERFECT TEST as used on the Hampshire Test, 10ft.6ins. and 11ft.:£5/-; the DRIVER PERFECTION: £4/4s. and so on down to the lowest price that a well-built, sound and reliable rod can be put on the market.

Other notable articles are spinning, trolling and prawning rods, salmon and trout reels, sea winches, sea rods, patent and improved landing rings and nets, creels, lines, gut casts, spinning baits etc., not forgetting Hardy's patent spear point hooks. An inspection of the firm's stall will reveal many other new and interesting features in tackle and appliances.

Hardy 'Super Silex' multiplier.

Hardy 'Jock Scott' multiplying reel, which came in a wooden box complete with a folding line winder (BELOW), and cork arbour used to decrease the capacity of the drum when using light lines.

So far the impression might have been given that Hardy's made only rods, and it was indeed the manufacture of rods that dominated the company's output in the early years. Contemporary catalogues reveal that few reels were produced and those which did appear were hardly distinguishable from others being produced all over Europe. They were generally hard metal and brass bronzed reels, incorporating in their designs materials such as ebonite for the reel plates for the sake of lightness. The 1888 catalogue included only two pages of reels out of a total of 120 pages.

Hardy's appeared to be slow in recognizing the importance of the reel market and it was not until three other brothers, Robert, Charles and Forster, joined the company at about the turn of the century, that the position changed. Forster Hardy was trained as a marine engineer and it was his influence which was largely responsible for changing the company's attitude to the manufacture of reels at Alnwick. He was later to move to the Pall Mall premises. Once the company had the reel market in its sights it was entirely in character that it should set out to capture it. This was done almost at a stroke with the introduction of the celebrated Perfect Reel in 1891.

The Perfect was described in the 1891 catalogue: 'It is perfectly ventilating, and, so far as possible, assists in drying

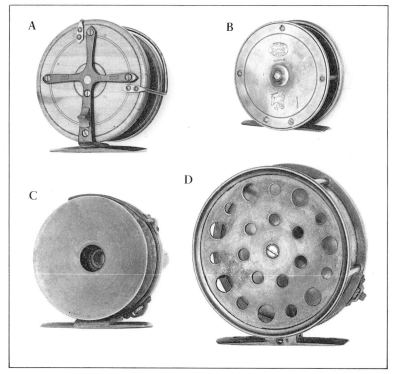

A: *a Hardy 'Nottingham' starback reel constructed of walnut and brass, with a horn handle. It is also fitted with a Bickerdyke line guide. The fact that it is marked 'Hardy's' makes it all the more important to the collector.* **B:** *a Hardy's 3⅛th contracted 'Field' reel.* **C:** *A rare example of the 1891 model 'Perfect' fly reel.* **D:** *Hardy's 1896 pattern all-brass 'Perfect'.*

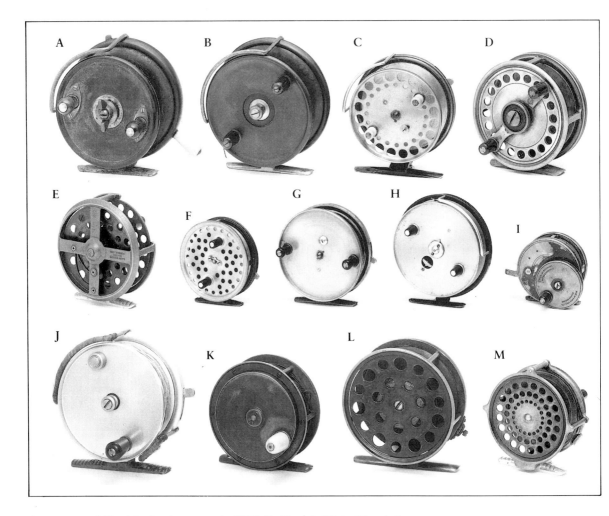

A: *an unusual Hardy's ebonite 'Silex' reel.* B: *Hardy's 'Ebona' sea fishing reel, the backplate and drum are constructed of ebonite.* C: *a fine example of a special order wide-drum frameless casting reel, marked as a Silex No. 2. Hardy's would build or adapt any of their reels to suit their customer's requirements.* D: *the Hardy 'Fortuna' fly reel. The adjustable silent brake fitted to this reel was the invention of Mr H. Andreas of New Zealand, and enabled the pressure of the brake to be altered, while playing a fish, as the handle of the reel remained stationary.* E: *a Hardy 'St George Tournament' fly reel. This is one of only three that were made, all built in 1938.* F: *Hardy's 3½ in. 'Eureka' reel, the ideal reel for bottom fishing and grayling float fishing.* G: *the Hardy 'Wallis' trolling reel.* H: *the Hardy 'Conquest' trolling reel.* I: *a Hardy 'Super Silex' multiplier.* J: *a Hardy 4½ in. 'Longstone' reel. Hardy's suggested it as a good reel for anglers who are always on the move and were uncertain of the sort of fishing they would encounter.* K: *Hardy's 4 in. bronzed brass 'Hercules' salmon reel with raised winding plate and ivory handle, from the late 1880s.* L: *Hardy's 1896 pattern bronzed brass 'Perfect' fly reel.* M: *the 'Bouglé' lightweight fly reel, by Hardy's.*

XI *A very rare collection of nineteenth-century Hardy reels.*

XII *An 1891 patent 2¹/₂ in. Hardy 'Perfect' fly reel.*

XIII *A 4¹/₂ in. Hardy 'Hercules' reel.*

XIV *A Hardy copper cast box and salmon flies.*

TOP: *the 'Silex' 4½ in. spinning reel by Hardy's.* MIDDLE: *a Hardy 'Silex Major' 4 in. reel.* ABOVE: *An extremely rare original model, of Hardy's brass 'Perfect' fly reel. It is a 3½ in. version of the 1891 pattern, with 'Hardy's Pat. No. 18373-612 Alnwick' engraved around the central core.*

the line. It has a regulating check and, running on ball bearings, is almost frictionless. It can be taken to pieces to clean instantly without any mechanical knowledge or tools.' The distinctive feature about the Perfect was its ball-bearing action, whereas the American Precision reels were largely modelled on the principles of watchmaking in the use of jewelled bearings. It was the first in a long line of different types of reels and their variants, which were to become world famous and unsurpassed by any major manufacturing company. Following the Perfect, other famous fly reels included the Bougle, Uniqua, St George, St John and Sunbeam, followed by the L.R.H. Range. Further notable spinning reels included the Silex, Eureka, Altex, Jock Scott and Elarex. The legendary Zane Grey led a group of big game reels which also included the Fortuna, the Alma, reel invented by C. Alma Baker, the Hardy-White-Wickham and the Sea Silex.

Zane Grey, apart from his international reputation as a writer of 'Wild West' novels, was also a pioneer of big game fishing. During the late 1920s he commissioned Hardy's to design for him the best big game outfit which money could buy. The reel was constructed of monel, a non-ferrous metal of phenomenal strength and ability to withstand the corrosive action of both sea and air. The accompanying rod was made of a combination of palakona cane and hickory with steel centre. The tackle was tried and tested and, thus equipped, Zane Grey proved it by capturing yet more records. In New Zealand he established a world record for a catch in one day by landing ten fish, each weighing over 250 pounds, and on the same day caught the largest ever fish on a rod and line, a Black Marlin weighing 976 pounds. In 1931 he broke his own record with the Hardy tackle by landing a Great Tahitian Striped Marlin which weighed 1,040 pounds after having lost 150 to 200 pounds to sharks as it was being reeled in.

The Zane Grey tackle went into general production until the war in 1939, and again for a short period after the war. It is not true, however, to claim that no other contemporary reels could compare with the Hardy production. Some American companies made exquisite reels which could more than hold their own with any of the period, but they were produced in very restricted quantities. These limited productions are, of course, highly desirable to the collector and are necessarily expensive because of their rarity. The Hardy reels are popular, not only for their quality, but since most models were made in substantial quantities, for their availability at a reasonable cost — with some notable exceptions!

CHAPTER SEVEN

Manufacturers and their catalogues

THROUGHOUT THE HISTORY of the sport, writers have contributed to an ever-growing body of literature describing virtually every facet of the angler's feelings towards his sport, as well as copious technical instruction on how to prepare the tackle and catch the fish. There is, however, only a very small amount of literature on the tackle manufacturers and their important part in the development of the sport. They are themselves somewhat to blame for this because, in common with most other specialist manufacturers, they seldom thought it worthwhile to preserve records or items which had ceased to interest the market. Often even the most basic information about the companies themselves was not recorded, or even thought of, until it was beyond recall. So it is that such information has to be gleaned from the few sources available, and little is available before the closing years of the nineteenth century when the tackle manufacturing industry began to undergo a major change in its organization.

While tackle manufacture was in the form of a cottage industry or, in some respects, a do-it-yourself business under the direction of many contemporary writers, little regard was paid to the individual makers. Not until the demand for ready-made tackle increased, and either the small-time manufacturers expanded, amalgamated or disappeared from the scene, did makers reach a prominence which can be traced in any detail. How they worked, what they produced and in what quantities, remained shrouded in obscurity until a wider public took up the sport and specialist periodicals were established to keep them informed and entertained.

The *Fishing Gazette* was prominent among such publications and, in its issue of the 28th March 1896, gives us a detailed description of David Slater's new factory at Newark-on-Trent. Slater had begun in business by supplying local bottom anglers fishing in the Nottingham tradition. He is an excellent example of a manufacturer who caught the

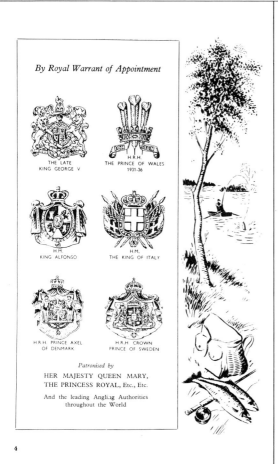

Within the illustration:

By Royal Warrant of Appointment

THE LATE
KING GEORGE V

H.R.H.
THE PRINCE OF WALES
1931-36

H.M.
KING ALFONSO

H.M.
THE KING OF ITALY

H.R.H. PRINCE AXEL
OF DENMARK

H.R.H. CROWN
PRINCE OF SWEDEN

Patronised by
HER MAJESTY QUEEN MARY,
THE PRINCESS ROYAL, Etc., Etc.

And the leading Angling Authorities
throughout the World

4

HARDY BROTHERS LIMITED

Important to Sportsmen

What's in a name ?

A man is known and judged by the reputation which his name enjoys. In the fishing world the name of HARDY stands supreme and the reputation which the name enjoys amongst anglers is second to none.

The name of HARDY stands as a symbol of many years' expert manufacturing experience, a wide knowledge of angling, personal superintendence and an unrivalled knowledge of the selection and suitability of equipment.

Eighty years' experience

In 1872 we commenced business as engineers and FISHING ROD AND TACKLE MAKERS. For over eighty years we have given to the angler not only the benefit of our experience as expert manufacturers but the knowledge gained by a family of accomplished anglers. From boyhood the present directors have been enthusiastic trout and salmon anglers and consequently have been able to bring this practical knowledge of the sport to assist in the manufacture of the equipment. They have fished regularly in the British Isles, Ireland, Canada, Norway and are familiar with most rivers in Europe. The construction of rods, reels, lines, flies, etc, carried out in our works are personally tested and perfected

on the river. From this dual standpoint we can offer a service to the angler quite unequalled in the trade.

Personal superintendence

Our whole attention has been given to the manufacture of fishing tackle and many important improvements introduced by us are widely known and acknowledged.

Mr L. R. Hardy, our Managing Director, has a practical knowledge of the various needs of the angler extending to some fifty years. His system of selecting, treating bamboos and making them into fishing rods has made Hardy's PALAKONA (Regd Trademark) split bamboo rods the best in the world and a boon to anglers. Himself an expert fisherman, he has an extensive knowledge of angling in all its various branches and is undoubtedly one of the leading authorities on the sport today.

Messrs Fred, Alan and Wm. F. Hardy, Directors and Managers, are also keen and experienced anglers and they have brought their experience gained as practical fishermen into the manufacture of Hardy tackle. Mr Wm. F. Hardy, the most recent acquisition to the Board, is already proving himself a keen fisherman and is spending a considerable amount of his time experimenting with and improving our tackle.

5

The frontispiece from an early 1950s Hardy catalogue, showing the extent of their royal patronage.

tide of development and expanded his production, avoiding the fate of many of his contemporaries who sank without trace. The *Gazette* clearly felt that his latest factory was worthy of note and regarded him as a leader in the field.

Situated in the centre of the celebrated malting town, almost within 'casting' distance of the fine old spire of the church of St. Mary Magdalene, it cannot fail to attract the attention of the passer-by, the steady and continued 'jet' 'jet' of the large engine being an indicator that cannot be misunderstood, and must impress upon its listeners that powerful machinery is necessary even for the production of the angler's appliances.

Admirably constructed for the purpose for which it was intended it presents an imposing edifice — 120ft. long, 20ft. wide, and three storeys high. Entering the basement

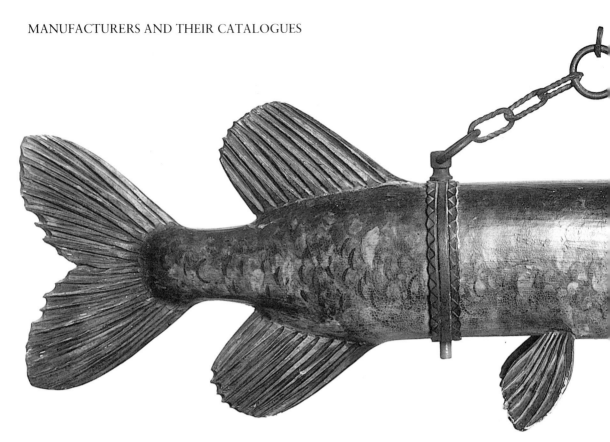

floor, the first thing to attract attention is the engine-room; and here constantly in motion is a powerful 10 horse power 'Otto' gas engine, of the latest design, and with all the recent additions patented by that eminent firm. Running almost the full length of the lower floor is a strong and powerful belting, driving the large circular saws, which are constantly employed roughing out timber for the manufacture of rods and reels, a tremendous stock of which — consisting of greenheart, lancewood, hickory, walnut, cherry, &c. — is always on hand. Here also will be observed several stacks of East Indian and other canes, whilst strewed about the floor are some thousands of reels, roughened out preparatory to their being placed in the seasoning room, for nothing, even of the cheapest make, is sent forth from the establishment but what will stand the critical examination of an expert as to its condition.

Ascending the second story, the first thing that attracts the eye is the admirably fitted-up office of the establishment, equal in dimensions alone almost to Mr Slater's original works; and here everything is carefully examined before being packed to be forwarded to its destination. And so admirably is this department managed by the staff, that although some hundreds of parcels are daily despatched, there is neither hurry nor bustle, showing that everything is under the supervision of a master mind. Leaving the office we enter the chief work-room of the factory, down the sides of which is a couple of lengths of shafting over 60ft. each, running as true and even as though it had been erected years instead of having only recently been placed in position, to which are connected the beltings of the various

One of a pair of painted wooden pike dating from the late nineteenth century which were probably used as shop signs. It was popular to hang these outside fishing tackle shops during the seventeenth, eighteenth and nineteenth centuries. Fletcher, a fishing tackle dealer in London during the seventeenth century, could be found at the sign of the Three Trouts, St Paul's, London.

lathes, &c.; and to give some idea of the quantity of belting in use, no less than 350 ft. is fixed in this room alone, whilst throughout the entire factory the length extends to 700 ft. On the right-hand side the rod makers are employed; and, though it would be invidious to mention any particular make, we may state that every variety, from the cheapest Nottingham roach rod up to the most exquisitely finished salmon rod, may be seen under process of manufacture. Here also are the metal stamping presses for the metal reel work — truly labour-saving machines — without which it would be scarcely possible to complete the enormous orders that are constantly being received for this speciality. On the opposite side are the benches occupied by the reel makers, and hours might be interestingly spent in observing the fine mechanism and ingenuity displayed in their production. Whether they be of wood, brass, ebonite, or aluminium the same care is displayed, every part being beautifully finished, and worthy of the high eulogium so frequently passed on Mr Slater's reels. Rod fittings, Slater's Patent Cage for Reels, and a variety of other necessaries are also produced in this department, to attempt to enumerate a tithe of which would occupy a far greater space than can be devoted to a brief notice of the establishment. Glancing overhead, the ceiling is festooned with large quantities of Nottingham reels in the rough, the ordinary seasoning room being inadequate to supply the extensive demand. At the further end of the second floor is the finishing room for the rods, and here the ladies are busily employed wrapping the same

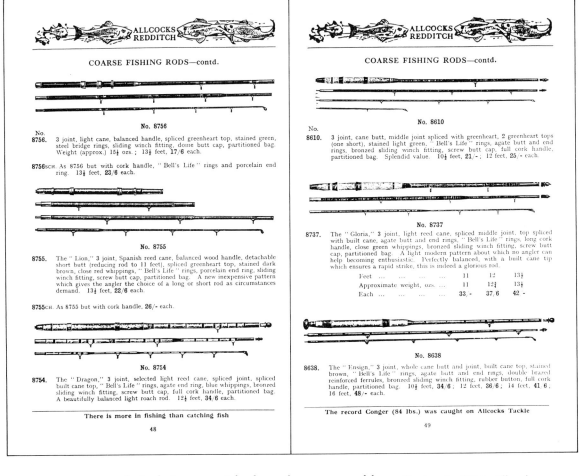

preparatory to their being varnished, making up tackle, and the many other light accomplishments requisite to complete an outfit.

The upper story embodies the show room and stores, and here at the present time is such an array of rods and reels as would astonish even those who have an intimate knowledge of Mr Slater's extensive business, and must be left to imagination, and from present appearances even the large factory now in use will require additions.

The information about themselves contained in the catalogues regularly published by the tackle manufacturers, and the descriptions of them by contemporary writers, offer not only an excellent background knowledge of the sport and its development but can be of great use in helping to identify and date specimens in the angler's collection.

Such company catalogues as have survived are now

During the 1930s Allcocks remained trade wholesalers, and published regular and extensive catalogues. In 1937 they were claiming to be the world's largest and oldest fishing tackle manufacturers.

becoming collector's pieces in their own right, and none more so than Hardy's, especially the earlier editions. Generally, early editions of company catalogues from about the middle of the nineteenth century to the 1880s, although rare, contain a limited amount of useful information. They are little more than lists of the items made or retailed by the company and contain few if any illustrations but, from them, the introduction of an item of tackle can be precisely dated, and its production life calculated from the number of editions in which it appears.

As the tackle industry progressed, the demand for catalogues grew among a public which looked more and more to the manufacturers for their tackle, both at home and abroad. The expanding empire rapidly extended the mail order business for the tackle industry. Catalogues developed from being mere lists to exhaustive arrays of the company's entire stock, profusely illustrated, and supplemented with highly technical information as to how, where and when to use the many items described. Well-known angling writers were often commissioned to contribute pieces, and testimonials also appeared from anglers all over the world.

Catalogues are, by their very nature, ephemeral. Each new edition supersedes the last and old copies are rare survivals. But the great variety of useful information and the excellent illustrations, especially those in colour which the later editions contained, tended to ensure that many copies were retained. These are now of both use and interest to the collector. The entries and illustrations provide an excellent source of reference but can lead to incorrect attribution. The appearance of an item in a catalogue may not necessarily mean that the piece was made by that firm. The firm issuing the catalogue may simply be the retailer and have either bought or commissioned the item from a specialist maker, merely impressing their own name and address on the piece. There is evidence to suggest that several items appearing concurrently in a number of catalogues originated from the same source.

By 1895 the tackle manufacturers were fully exploiting the potential of the catalogue. For the following 40 years the huge range of tackle is described and illustrated, with much detail about what each item was intended to achieve in practice in sea, coarse and game fishing. This is of inestimable value to the collector in identifying maker's marks, dates and the materials used, lengths of rods, types of reel, line, capacity, etc.

Company catalogues can also provide an interesting source

of information on the companies themselves, information which, if not published in this way, could easily have been lost. The 1926 edition of William Mills & Son's catalogue, published from their premises at 21 Park Place, New York, devotes the first page to a potted history of the firm from its establishment in 1822 to 1875, when it was taken over and given its present name. This catalogue also makes the point that Mills was the sole agent for H.L. Leonard's split bamboo rods at that time and that mail order was available world-wide, a significant fact for collectors of the Leonard rod.

One of the companies that dominated the manufacture of fishing tackle during the first half of this century was Allcock of Redditch. Their large operation spanned the world, with branches, offices and agencies based on one of the largest factories in the business, until its closure in the early 1960s. In its heyday Allcock's produced a formidable range of tackle which, in some instances, remains unsurpassed. The Allcock's Aeriel Fishing Reel has become a legend among anglers and is still much sought after for use. Although copies have been produced, none quite matches up to the original. The 1937/8 catalogue or 'Angler's Guide and Abridged List of Fishing Tackle' describes the firm as having been:

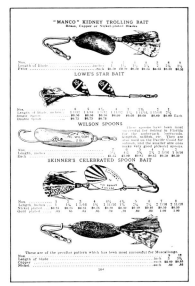

> ...founded by Mr Polycarp Allcock in 1803, 'when George III was King'. Thus we were making fishing tackle at Redditch before the Battle of Waterloo. The business was greatly expanded by his son, the late Mr Samuel Allcock, J.P., and has long enjoyed the distinction of being the largest manufacturer of Fishing Tackle in the World...
>
> Only the exceptional merit of Allcock's tackle has rendered possible the world-wide celebrity which it enjoys. At International Exhibitions the record of Grand Prix and Highest Awards won by Allcocks has never been equalled or approached by any other tackle manufacturer.

International exhibitions of commercial products of all kinds were an invention of the nineteenth century. Their popularity in the specialist field of fishing tackle can be gauged from the press comments made at the time of the 1896 Fisheries Exhibition, that the Royal Aquarium, Westminster, in which it had been held annually, was no longer large enough to cope with the great number of exhibitors and visiting public. Alternative accomodation would have to be sought in the Crystal Palace, 'where there would be an abundance of well lighted space in the building, and ample facilities for actually testing the casting pairs of rods on the ornamental waters close to the doors.'

Illustrations from the 1926 William Mills & Son's catalogue, showing the many useful and ingenious items available to the angler. A considerable part of Mills' business was done through mail order.

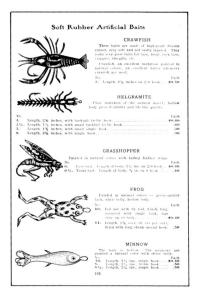

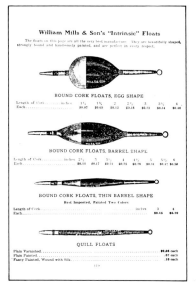

The press reviews of the various tackle exhibitions are veritable mines of information for the collector, with their detailed descriptions of manufacturers' ranges of output and comments on comparison and prices. They also provide an accurate picture of the manufacturing scene and the state of play between the major protagonists. *The Fishing Gazette* provides an interesting description of Henry Murton's stand at the 1896 Fisheries Exhibition at the Royal Aquarium:

Of 109, Grey-street, Newcastle, has an attractive show, both of fishing rods and tackle, and waterproof goods of all kinds for anglers. No one in these days can pretend that they cannot afford a good fishing rod when Mr Murton offers his 'Tyneside Fly Rod' made, he assured us, of seasoned greenheart, with one top and single braised, for three half-crowns; and you can get it double braised with two tops, at 11s. for a 10ft. rod, 12s.6d. for an 11ft., and 13s.6d. for a 12ft. The latter would be a good rod for artificial May Fly work. Among the rods we handled — we cannot say tried, for there is not space to swing a cat, much less a fly rod — were a very nice 20s. 15ft. grilse rod, an 18ft. salmon rod at 25s., not, of course, elaborately finished, but equal for fishing purposes to the same rod, double braised, with two tops, cork handle, &c., at £3. Then some 45s. whole cane fly rods, 14ft. to 16ft. We liked a £4 split-cane fly rod, also a ten guinea 18ft. split-cane steel centre rod, with lock joints &c. We would just as soon have the same rod without the steel centre at £8.8s., for we have never yet been able to satisfy ourselves that the steel centre is anything more than a 'passenger', as our boating friends say. Sea fishing is undoubtedly coming rapidly into fashion. Almost every exhibitor makes a feature of tackle and rods for it, and Mr Murton shows a well-made 15s. combination sea rod, and one of greenheart at 7s.6d. There is one feature about a 4½ins. salmon reel of Mr Murton's, called the 'New Break Reel', that you do not often find, and that is, of the two springs controlling the check one is considerably stronger than the other, so that a salmon pulling off line has to pull against a harder check than you do when you get a chance to wind him in — this is just as it should be.

Merton's development of the salmon reel was interesting because at that time most reels were fitted with only one spring, causing the tension to be identical whichever way the barrel or drum of the reel was turning. Consequently, by putting in a second spring, it was made more difficult for the fish to run against the ratchet or spring when winding it in. Despite frowning on the development of the steel centre rod, an innovation probably pioneered by Hardy's, the writer clearly approved of Merton's New Break salmon reel, for he continued:

> Among all the contrivances we have seen we know nothing for salmon fishing so safe as a good strong check, with cog wheels and pin of hardened steel — not too strong, of course. Reels are advertised with devices which will stop the hardest rush of a heavy salmon. Jock Scott! How we should like to see the inventor do it. Why he would be 'up a tree', and his rod and line too, in about five seconds. But Mr Murton's 'New Break Reel' is perfectly plain and perfectly sensible, and he guarantees the works to be hardened steel. Another reel we saw at Mr Murton's and other stalls was one with a very free running aluminium barrel, which by an ingenious contrivance can be disconnected from the handle. We hear they are selling well, a great many being bought by American visitors.

The writer goes on to review the Ogden Smith stand. This company was located in London at 6 Park Side, Hyde Park Corner, and at 71 St John's Hill, Clapham. Their more mundane range included whole cane rods at 30 shillings, and gun metal reels with the now customary hardened steel works.

Appendix 1 contains a schedule of British retailing and manufacturing companies from the seventeenth century to the present day. The schedule is arranged in alphabetical order together with their addresses and changes of address, where these appear in source material. Dates have also been included; where possible these state when the company was founded and when discontinued. Records are, however, very sketchy in their information, and often dates merely record a contemporary reference to the company. No other information about many of the companies included is at present available.

CHAPTER EIGHT

The artistic angle

WILLIAM JONES: Trout Fishing. *Painted around 1825, oil on canvas, 16×24in.*

IT CANNOT BE THE AIM of a mere chapter to cover a subject which might be more properly dealt with in a whole volume — and a sizeable one at that. British sporting art as a whole has been substantially covered in many books, but little has appeared on angling since W. Shaw Sparrow's elegant tome, *Angling in British Art* was published in 1922. Angling as a sport has, of course, inspired a copious library over a period of at least 300 years. Much of angling art has been produced to illustrate these works, creating a fascinating collector's field in itself and worthy of yet another book. It is, unfortunately, not in the brief of this one to stray into those tantalizing waters. A chapter can do little more than whet the appetite and stimulate further interest.

The essence of sporting art, and one of the great loves of

KILLED *on* WYE COURTFIELD WATER *10TH APRIL 1913* BY **E.F.M.B.** *Weight* 35½ LBS.

the British, is the sight of a well-bred animal either in action or in repose. The human element is almost always of secondary importance.

Since the seventeenth century, artists have been catering to the needs of huntin', shootin' and fishin' enthusiasts — and very much in that order. By far the senior branch of this peculiarly British art form centres around the horse. The considerable ballyhoo which attends all the equine sports has captured most of the artistic limelight. Some of the best-known figures in British art, both native and adopted, have made their names in this field. Proud studies of famous racehorses, with their equally proud owners and trainers in attendance, scenes of the pleasures and pitfalls of the field, and the excitement of the finishing post have been produced in prodigious quantities by artists both great and small.

Shootin' pictures have tended to come a rather poor second to the glories of the horse. Many sporting artists have wisely focused their attention on the next best thing to a horse, artistically speaking, the splendid gun dogs dashing full-tilt after hapless quarry or proudly standing guard over it at the end of a successful day.

And fishin'? Ballyhoo is the last thing an angler wants and angling artists have faced considerable difficulties. Peace and tranquillity are hard to reconcile with sporting art. The drama, when it does occur, is difficult to depict because most of it takes place out of sight. No doubt this branch of sporting art would have been taken more seriously had the anglers long ago abandoned their rods and taken to training osprey or herons to hunt the fish for them. However, as the sport has developed along quite different lines, angling artists have had to make the best of the limited resources available. Many have done well, some have triumphed.

Angling art has lived unobtrusively in its quiet backwater for quite as long as the other forms of sporting art. In fact it

A painted, carved wood, life-size salmon trophy by Hardy's.

JOHN RAPHAEL SMITH: The Angelic Angler. *One of a pair of mezzotints published by Robert Sayer, London, in 1787. Colour was added by hand. The lighthearted intent of the print is shown in the lines which appear with it:*

At once victorious, with your hands and eyes,
You make the fishes & the Men your Prize,
And while the pleasing Slavery we Court,
I fear you Captivate us both for Sport.

may lay claim to be the oldest form, since Francis Barlow, regarded as the first sporting artist, began to paint studies of birds and fish in the seventeenth century. In his attempt to overcome the inherent difficulties in his field, the artist of angling subjects has developed all the visible elements in the scene. Water, of course, is of primary importance and appears foaming and dashing, or flowing quietly with light playing upon its surface — or even with the lack of light required by the angler. The quarry in its natural habitat has frequently been prominent in sporting art and many angling artists have depicted the various sporting fish in naturalistic style to whet the appetite of the sportsman. The landscape also plays an important role in the picture, evoking memories of happy hunting grounds and successful bags.

Few artists have confined themselves exclusively to angling subjects, but many have touched upon them. No matter how diverse the talents of the artists, almost all of them have been active anglers themselves. Angling art has, therefore, a large number of exponents, some famous, some obscure.

Virtually the entire range of artistic media is available to the collector — oil painting, watercolour, etching, aquatint, lithograph and drawing. Angling pictures have also covered just about every category of subject. Landscapes abound, having the one necessary feature, a stretch of water over which toils the focal point of the piece. Seascapes are a relatively new addition to the repertoire, reflecting the upsurge of big game fishing as a sport from the end of the last century. Portrait painters, caricaturists, still life and nature study artists and, of course, sporting artists, have all added to the large and varied body of angling art.

With few exceptions, examples are available within a relatively modest price range. Not every angler, of course, will wish to form a definitive collection of pictures, but many will be delighted to discover their particular interest captured on canvas or paper. What more could an angler require from an artist than to be reminded of his deep pleasure in his sport at times when he is unable to indulge it, or to relive his triumphs by contemplating a study of his favourite fish — dead or alive.

The one category of sporting art which has produced angling artists *per se* is that of still life. During the first half of the nineteenth century British sporting art flowered and while most artists were devoted to equine subjects, a few were keen enough anglers themselves to concentrate on the smaller market for angling pictures.

Henry Alken (1785-1857) is the name that most readily springs to mind in this context. He was born in London to a family of Danish extraction which produced several sporting artists. Henry was a keen huntsman and became best known for his hunting pictures. It is probable that he also had more than a passing interest in angling for he painted quite a number of oils and watercolours of the angler in action. In common with many artists, and not just those concerned with sport, Alken was keen to boost his income with the production of engravings. While the oil paintings were available only to a restricted and affluent market, a factor which remains unchanged, a much wider market could be reached through the much cheaper and more plentiful engraved image. At first Alken published his engravings anonymously under the pseudonym Ben Tally Ho. After

JOHN MEQUINER: Portrait of John Gervase Howard Marsh, *aged eight, with landing net and creel; 36×28in., signed (detail).*

about 1820 the quality of his work declined to the point that his reputation was irretrievably damaged and he died in poverty in 1851.

James Pollard (1792-1867) was also exclusively a sporting artist and has always been popular for his coaching scenes. He produced many hunting, racing, steeplechasing and shooting pictures; in common with Alken, he also reached a wider and ready market with his engravings. Pollard is known to have been a keen angler and he painted several scenes of anglers in landscapes, depicted with great accuracy if not with the highest quality of technique.

Lone anglers, standing almost motionless beside a peaceful stretch of water, have become a part of the landscape. Countless artists have been grateful to use them in their compositions to enliven the scene, as a welcome alternative to the overworked drover herding cattle, or the tireless old woman gathering faggots. Landscape painting in Britain has become populated with anglers desporting themselves on bridges or quietly getting on with the job in the distance beside, on, or in the water.

The great J.M.W. Turner, a keen angler and a member of the exclusive Houghton Fishing Club, included anglers on both land and water in his pictures. John Sell Cotman, Peter de Wint, David Cox and William Muller are among the other major British painters of the nineteenth century to have used anglers to give figurative interest to their pictures of the British landscape. John Constable painted one of the most delightful studies of a child's pleasure in angling in his well-known work *The Young Waltonians*. Both James Stark and Edmund Bristow frequently included anglers in views of the Thames around Windsor. Among the minor figures in the nineteenth century who painted what might be called 'angling landscapes', a William Jones often appears, flourishing from about 1825 to 1850. Little is known about him, and indeed there may well be more than one artist with the name, but the style was very much of the Constable school. Another noted landscape painter who also produced several good angling pictures was Thomas Barker of Bath (1769-1847). In all these paintings by landscape artists the angler appears more or less as a prop to help provide a peaceful and pastoral atmosphere and a focal point to the composition. When is a landscape an angling picture? It is not easy to say and there is no precise definition. A river landscape may appeal to an angler just as much without a figure as with one.

However, in many instances, more than a passing concern in angling is worked into the picture. With the increased interest in angling which developed with the passing of the nineteenth century, the angler takes more than a prop role in the picture. Richard Ansdell RA was a Liverpool artist, influenced in his style by Edwin Landseer and J.F. Herring. He produced many landscapes set in the Highlands, then becoming increasingly fashionable under the influence of Queen Victoria and Prince Albert. His pictures feature fine and exact studies of animals, or parties of huntsmen or anglers with the kill. Charles Martin Hardie RA, a Scottish artist, typifies the angling landscape painter of the latter years of the nineteenth century, with the angler featured undisturbed in a perfect setting.

It was to C.M. Hardie that Julius Drew turned for his portrait at about the turn of the century. Drew was the wealthy proprietor of a chain of stores, now famed for his commission, just prior to the First World War, to Sir Edwin Lutyens to build the remarkable Castle Drogo in Devon, the last of the great country houses. Hardie depicts his client at his Scottish property, Faskally in Perthshire, in full fishing rig, having just landed a fine salmon. Both the portrait and the now stuffed salmon can be seen at Castle Drogo.

It is, perhaps, stretching a point to describe portraits as angling pictures even though the sitter is obviously anxious to demonstrate that angling is his favourite pastime. Such eminent artists as John Zoffany and Arthur Devis painted clients with their rods, but the vast sums such pictures would now make have nothing to do with their angling content. They are of interest to anglers if contemporary engravings of them are available.

Caricaturists are always quick to spot and exploit the humour in a situation and angling appears to have escaped

BELOW LEFT: HENRY ALKEN: Ideas Accidental and Incidental to Hunting, and other Sports: caught in Leicestershire!. *From a set of hand-coloured engravings, published by Thomas McLean, London 1830.*

BELOW RIGHT: SIR ROBERT FRANKLAND: Delights of Fishing. *From a set of six hand-coloured etchings with aquatint, engraved & published by Charles Turner, London 1823.*

XV HENRY ALKEN SNR.: On the Avon at Fordingbridge, *6½ × 8¾ in.*

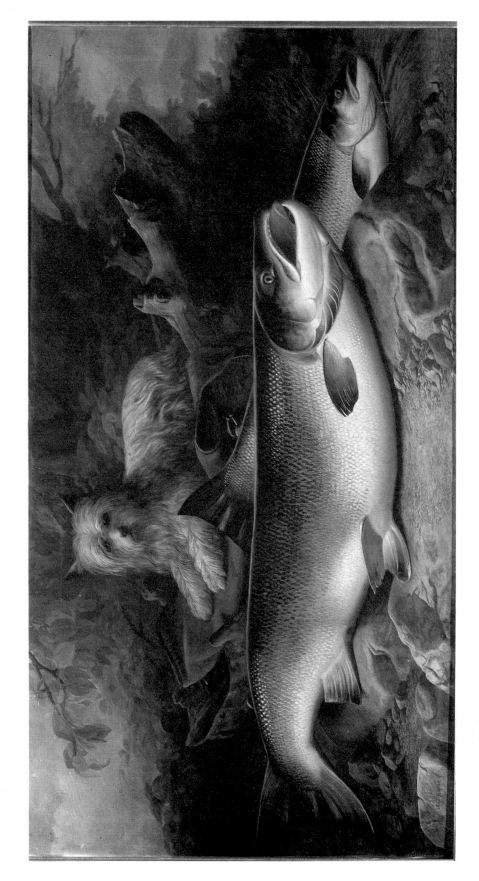

XVI JOHN RUSSELL.: Still life with salmon and terrier.

A life-size salmon trophy by Farlow's, of carved wood. Inscribed 'C.T. June 18th 1910 39 lbs'.

the attention of very few of them. From the great satirists of the eighteenth century, such as Thomas Rowlandson and James Gillray, throughout the nineteenth century with such figures as George Cruikshank, John Doyle and the cartoonists of *Punch*, John Leech and Charles Keene, into this century with Heath Robinson — all either poked fun gently or used the medium to lambast the unfortunate objects of their attention. Caricatures and cartoons are of especial interest to the angling collector as they were generally published in quantities and a good collection can still be formed.

So far it would seem that only anglers have appeared in the art. Far from it. The fish themselves have always been the most popular subjects, both dead and alive, and fish pictures comprise the largest category in angling art. They are probably also the most readily available to the collector.

'Still life' is a curious term for describing a study of death. It is used, of course, to describe studies of all kinds of immobile objects, but perhaps the French *nature morte* is more accurate. As already mentioned, Francis Barlow painted still life pictures of fish, as well as of other game, during the second half of the seventeenth century. A very few artists continued the genre in the eighteenth century, notably Stephen Elmer of Farnham, who established a tradition which was to burgeon in the next century. His studies of a day's catch, arranged on a bank with a creel or as a foreground to

JOHN RUSSELL: A Brace of Fresh Run Hen Salmon on the Banks of a Sea Loch. *Typical of the 'scaly portrait' painted soon after the catch, with landscape added later. This type of still life was popular from the last quarter of the eighteenth century until ousted by photography at the end of the nineteenth; oil on canvas, 17½×34½in., c.1870, signed*

a wider view, inspired a style which can be found flourishing virtually unchanged at least a century later. With the rise in popularity of the sport arose in parallel the demand for pictures of a particularly good day's catch. Towards the end of the last century many artists, about whom little is known, are recorded as painters of fish. Even the master exponent of the type, Henry Leonidas Rolfe, remains something of a shadowy figure. He exhibited at the Royal Academy for more than 25 years, from 1847 to 1874, and was described by a contemporary writer as 'the celebrated limner of scaley portraits'. Business for these painters of fish was brisk and they could not afford to be leisurely because the subject had to be depicted while still at its best.

Pictures of fish in their natural habitat had largely taken the place of still lifes, although many artists in the last century were adept at both. Some could be quite amusing, but with the development of a greater awareness of the environment and the passing of Victorian sentimentality, studies of fish *au naturel* become more true to life. The early twentieth century passion, etching, produced fine images of fish, especially the leaping salmon, which are still not beyond the means of the 'modest' collector.

There is a strong element of the 'trophy' about the still life painting of fish, and this is the whole purpose of the stuffed and mounted fish. Taxidermy, of course, is an ancient art and the stuffed fish is not the invention of the Victorians, as is evident in these lines from Shakespeare's *Romeo and Juliet*, Act V, Scene 1:

'I do remember an apothecary, —
And hereabouts he dwells, - whom late I noted
In tatter'd weeds, with overwhelming brows,
Culling of simples; meagre were his looks,
Sharp misery had worn him to the bones:
And in his needy shop a tortoise hung,
An alligator stuff'd, and other skins
Of ill-shaped fishes ...'

A French work on taxidermy, giving directions on the proper method of preserving fish, appeared in 1758; many more followed in the next century. Domed cases containing pretty coloured birds might adorn the parlour, but a fine stuffed fish in a bow-fronted glass case was sure to grace the study. Nor was it complete without being inscribed with the weight of the fish, the river from which it was caught, the date and, of course, the name of the person who caught it, in gilt lettering on the glass.

HENRY JERVIS ALFRED: King of the Pool. *Alfred painted fish, both dead and alive, and also wrote about angling. His family kept a tackle shop in Moorgate, London; oil on canvas, 6×8½in., signed and dated 1881.*

The doyen of the art was J. Cooper of London. While many taxidermists in all parts of Britain included the mounting of fish, Cooper alone made a speciality of it. His business began in the 1870s and continued into the 1950s, maintaining a prodigious output. He and many other taxidermists marked their cases with trade labels. Twenty years ago a stuffed fish could be bought for less than a fresh one, but no longer: Victorian taxidermy has risen high in the collector's estimation.

At the same time there was a substantial market for plaster-cast fish models, painted and preserved to look just like the real thing. To the angler there was never any question as to which was superior — it had to be the actual fish. Moulded plaster and carved wood models, however, were popular as trophies. *The Fishing Gazette* of 1887 mentions those on display at the International Fisheries Exhibition made by Frank Buckland and painted by Rolfe, Searl and others.

The following list includes the names of artists whose works are more or less of angling interest. Some are well known and need no futher description here: others are as yet obscure and known only from exhibition lists or a few pictures which have appeared on the market:

ADAMS, DOUGLAS *fl.*1880-1905. Landscapes in oils and fishing prints.

ALFRED, HENRY JERVIS *fl.*1855-83. Angling writer from family of tackle retailers in London. Fine oils of still life and studies of fish in natural habitat.

ALKEN, HENRY (Snr) 1785-1851. Sporting artist including some angling oils and watercolours. Set of three illustrations for his quarto on British Sports, 'Pike', 'Salmon' and 'Fishing in a Punt' engraved by J. Clark and published by T. McLean in January 1820 and again in 1824, in two sizes, with the back printed in colour and the foreground by hand. Others include 'Fly Fishing Difficulties' and 'Bottom Fishing'.

ANSDELL, RICHARD RA. 1815-1885. Liverpool sporting and animal painter in the style of Landseer and Herring; fine Highland landscapes with anglers.

APPLEBEE, LEONARD ARCA. 1914- . Exhibited RA 1956-64, oils.

BARKER, THOMAS 1769-1847. Bath landscape artist, with anglers often included.

BARKER, BENJAMIN 1776-1838. Brother of Thomas, landscapes.

BARLOW, FRANCIS 1626-1704. Large-scale oils of birds and game, including fish, commissioned for country houses, also etchings — 'River Fishing', 'Salmon Fishing' and 'Angling', etched by W. Hollar, from a series on British Sports; also one angling plate from a series for *Aesop's Fables*.

BARNARD, EDWARD 1785-1861. Landscapes.

BARRAUD, WILLIAM 1810-50. Sporting pictures, occasionally of angling interest.

BARRINGTON-BROWNE, W.E. Living angling artist, anglers in landscapes.

BARTLETT, WILLIAM ROI, RBA *fl.*1874-93.

BATEMAN, JAMES 1815-49. London sporting artist, some fishing scenes and illustrations.

BATES, DAVID Exhibited 1868-93. Worcester landscape artist with anlgers.

BAYES, ALFRED WALTER *fl.*1858-1903. Exhibited RA. Landscapes and figures in oils, etchings.

BECKWITH, H. *fl.*1832-54. Engravings and watercolours.

BEDDINGTON, ROY 1910- . Illustrations and landscapes.

BELL, EDWARD *fl.*Worcester 1811-47. Still life game, fish, landscape and genre; engravings and mezzotints.

BESTOESMITH, W. *fl.*Sudbury, 1836. Still life, fish.

BOSTOCSMITH, C.V. *fl.* late nineteenth century. Still life, fish.

BOULDING, G. Illustrations.

BRACKETT, W. Exhibited Great Fisheries Exhibition.

BRIGGS, ERNEST RI. 1866-1913. Scottish artist noted for angling landscapes; wrote and illustrated *Angling and Art in Scotland*.

BRISTOW, EDMUND 1787-1876. Landscapes around Windsor, oils and engravings.

CALLCOTT, SIR AUGUSTUS WALL RA. 1779-1844. Landscapes in oil.

CARLESS, FRANK *fl.*Sussex 1904-5.

CARRICK, JOHN MULCASTER Exhibited 1854-78. Anglers in landscape.

CHAMBERLAIN, MISS E *fl.*1816. Fish.

CHILD, JOHN M. *fl.*Dudley 1828. Fish.

COLLIER, J.H. *fl.* late nineteenth century. Still life with fish and tackle.

COLLINS, WILLIAM RA. 1788-1847. Landscape artist, two paintings of children angling engraved.

COMBER, MISS MARY E. *fl.* late nineteenth century. Of Warrington, fish.

CONSTABLE, JOHN 1776-1837. 'The Young Waltonians', mezzotint engraved by David Lucas.

COOPER, CLAUDE *fl.* late nineteenth century. Animals and fish.

COURSELLES-DUMONT, HENRI *fl.* late nineteenth century. London, fishing.

CRUIKSHANK, GEORGE 1792-1878. Caricaturist, 'Angling a la Mode'.

CUMMINS, W.J. *fl.* late nineteenth century. Proprietor of North of England Rod Works, Bishop Auckland; included his own sketches in his tackle catalogue.

DADD, FRANK RI. 1851-1929. Sporting artist, worked for *Illustrated London News & Graphic*, woodcuts.

DAGLEY, RICHARD *fl.*1785-1841. Figure painter, etchings.

DAVIS, MISS CELIA *fl.* late nineteenth century, York. Landscapes and fish.

DEVIS, ARTHUR 1711-87. Portraits, some sitters with fishing rods.

DOCHARTY, JAMES ARSA. 1829-78. Glasgow landscape artist.

DOYLE, JOHN 1797-1868. Political cartoons.

DUBE, MADAME MATHE *fl.* late nineteenth century, Paris. Fish.

EARL, GEORGE *fl.*1856-83. London sporting artist.

EDWARDS, EDWIN 1823-79. Exhibited RA. 1861-79. Landscapes, seascapes and etchings around London, especially Sunbury.

ELIOT, GRANVILLE *fl.* late nineteenth century, Horsham, Sussex. Fishing.

ELMER, STEPHEN ARA. 1717-96. Farnham artist specializing in animals, birds, dogs, still life and dead game, including fish.

FAIRMAN, C. *fl.* late nineteenth century. Still life, fish.

FIELDING, NEWTON 1799-1856. Landscapes and aquatints of angling interest.

FRANKLAND, SIR ROBERT 1784-1849. Sporting engravings and aquatints. Set of six amusing fishing scenes aquatinted by Charles Turner and published by Turner & Thomas McLean in 1823.

GEAR, J. *fl.*1815-21, London. Sea-pieces, two sets of aquatints.

GEDDES, WILLIAM *fl.* mid-nineteenth century. Scottish, of Blairgowrie; still life of fish and tackle.

GILES, JAMES WILLIAM RSA. 1801-70. Aberdeen; landscapes, animals and sporting, especially angling — still life in the Highlands.

GILLRAY, JAMES 1757-1815. Caricaturist with a few caricatures of angling interest.

GRIZET, ERNEST *fl.* late nineteenth century. Commended in *The Fishing Gazette* 1887 for paintings of fish.

HADEN, SIR FRANCIS SEYMOUR *fl.*1865-85. Series of angling etchings.

HAGBE, LOUIS PRI. 1806-85. Belgian; lithographs after Landseer.

HAINES, MISS AGNES ELIZA *fl*.London 1887. Fish.

HAMILTON, WILLIAM RA. 1751-1801. Charming 'Boudoir Realism', engraved by Bartolozzi and A. Cardon.

HANKES, J.F. *fl*.1838-59. Oils.

HARDY, CHARLES *fl*.1815. Illustrator: Trophies of angling for *The Angler's Guide, 1815*.

HARDIE, CHARLES MARTIN ARSA. Edinburgh artist, good angling landscapes and anglers. Exhibited RA. 1880-91.

HEATH, HENRY *fl*.1835-50. Set of six lithographs, all of fishing, published by Baily in 1835.

HEATH, JAMES ARA 1757-1834. Engravings.

HEATH, WILLIAM 1795-1840. Scottish fishing scenes lithographed.

HEMY, CHARLES NAPIER 1841-1917. Paintings of sea fishing and landscapes.

HILTON, WILLIAM RA. 1786-1839. Nottingham, fishing scenes engraved by H.R. Cook.

HOFLAND, THOMAS CHRISTOPHER 1777-1843. Landscape artist; wrote and illustrated *Angler's Guide*, 1839.

HOLDITCH, J. *fl*.London 1785. Fish.

HOOK, JAMES CLARK RA. 1819-1907. Seascapes and landscapes, keen angler, often painted children angling.

HORMANN, THOEDORE DE *fl*.Vienna late nineteenth century. Fishermen.

HOWITT, SAMUEL 1750-1822. Sporting artist, illustrations *Anglers Manual* a set of four line engravings: 'Minnow', 'Worm', 'Fly', and 'Pike', published 1798-9 and later coloured.

HUGHES, MISS F.L. *fl*.London 1884. Fish.

HUME, MRS THOMAS *fl*.Hampshire 1862-1906. Painting of general fishing subjects.

HUNTER, COLIN ARA, RI, RSW. 1841-1904. Scottish fishing subjects.

INSKIPP, JAMES 1790-1868. Landscape and genre painter with angling interest; illustrated Sir Harris Nicholas's edition of Walton's *The Compleat Angler*, 1833-6. Exhibited RA. and British Institute.

JONES, RICHARD 1767-1840. Reading artist — few mezzotints of angling scenes by Charles Turner for Ackermann.

JONES, WILLIAM *fl*.1825-47. One of about eight of a family of artists; oils and illustrations for Ackermann.

JURY, JULIUS 1821-70. Paintings and illustrations for *The Fisherman's Magazine*.

KELL, W.F. *fl*.London 1875. Still life, fish and tackle, landscapes.

KNIGHT, A. ROWLAND *fl*.1900-05. Oil studies of fish in natural habitat.

LANE, THEODORE Exhibited London 1816-30. Interiors, 'The Enthusiast', an amusing angling engraving.

LEE, FREDERICK RICHARD RA. 1798-1879. Landscapes of fishing interest.

LEECH, JOHN 1817-64. Illustrations and cartoons.

LODGE, GEORGE EDWARD Exhibited 1881-1917. Scottish landscapes with anglers.

LOVERGROVE, H. *fl*.High Wycombe 1829-44. Landscapes and fish studies.

LUBER, A. *fl*.Berlin late nineteenth century. Fish.

MACALLUM, HAMILTON 1841-96. Scottish watercolour landscapes, coastal figures.

MACBETH, ROBERT WALKER 1848-1910. Still life, fish, pastoral landscape, genre and etchings.

McKEWAN, DAVID HALL 1817-73. Pupil of David Cox, landscapes of angling interest.

MACLAGEN, PHILIP DOUGLAS *b*.1901. Figures and landscape, still life of tackle.

MACWHIRTER, JOHN 1839-1911. Landscapes of angling interest, worked in Europe and America.

MOLE, JOHN HENRY 1814-86. Watercolour landscapes of angling interest.

MORLAND, GEORGE 1760-1804. Noted genre painter; series of local fishermen painted in Isle of Wight in 1799, also a pair of mezzotints: 'A

Party Angling' and 'The Anglers Repast', engraved by his brother-in-law William Ward and published by J.R. Smith in 1780, reissued in colour by G. Keating in 1789. Also coloured mezzotint 'Children Fishing' engraved by P.Dawe, 1788.

MURDOCH, W.G. BURN Exhibited 1882-1919. Illustrations.

NEW, EDMUND HORT 1871-1931. Illustrations and etchings.

NICHOL, ERSKINE RA. 1825-1904. An accomplished angler, painted several good angling pictures.

OFFORD, J.J. *fl.*1880. Fish still life.

OVENDON, T *fl.*1817-32. Studies of fish in landscape.

POLLARD, JAMES 1792-1867. Well known for coaching scenes and sporting pictures; keen angler; angling pictures, many engraved either by himself, his father Robert Pollard, J. Harris, R Havell and others.

POLLARD, ROBERT 1755-1838. Father of James; engravings of angling interest.

POLLOCK, M.R. *fl.* late nineteenth century. Still life, fish.

REINAGLE, PHILIP RA. 1749-1833. Sporting painter, some fishermen in coloured engravings by J. Hassell and W. Nicholls, published by Hassell and T. Richards 1814.

REYNOLDS, FRANK 1876-?. Illustrator for *Punch*, *Sketch* and *Illustrated London News*.

ROBINSON, WILLIAM HEATH 1872-1944. Caricatures.

ROLFE, ALEXANDER *fl.*1839-71. Landscape, still life and sporting subjects, especially angling.

ROLFE, EDMUND *fl.*1830-47. Landscapes, still life and many angling subjects.

ROLFE, F. *fl.*1849-53. Studies of fish.

ROLFE, HENRY LEONIDAS *fl.*1847-81. Exhibited RA. 1847-74, a prolific painter of still life of fish and tackle, and studies of fish in natural habitat.

ROTH, GEORGE *fl.*1810-15. Studies of fish in landscapes.

ROWLANDSON, THOMAS 1756-1827. Caricaturist; two of angling interest: 'Anglers near a Watermill' and 'A Snug Angling Party'.

RUSSELL, JOHN *fl.c.*1870. Studies of fish, still life and angling subjects.

SADLER, WALTER DENDY RBA. 1854-1923. Costume pieces, occasionally of angling interest, much engraved.

SARGENT, JOHN SINGER 1856-1925. Visit to Norway in 1901 produced three fine fishing pictures and several studies.

SMITH, JOHN RAPHAEL 1752-1812. Fishing subjects in the 'Boudoir Realism' style, published by Robert Sayer & J. Bennett 1781.

STARK, JAMES River scenes on the Thames with anglers.

SURTEES, JOHN 1819-1915. Landscapes.

SUSINI Commended highly in the *Fishing Gazette* of 1887 for still life of fish.

TUNNICLIFFE, CHARLES FREDERICK 1901- Animals, birds and fish, watercolour and etching.

TURNER, JOSEPH MALLORD WILLIAM 1775-1851. Several landscapes including anglers engraved.

WALKER, A. 1726-65. Fishing subjects in the 'Boudoir Realism' style, engraved by T. Wilson 1771.

WALLS, WILLIAM RSA. 1860-1942. Scottish animal painter.

WHYMPER, CHARLES RI. 1853-1941. Oils and watercolours of animals, sport, landscape and genre. Illustrator, etchings of shooting and fishing. Exhib. RA. from 1852.

WILKINSON, NORMAN 1878-1971. Marine and angling landscapes and etchings.

WOLSTENHOLME, Jr. 1798-1883.

ZOFFANY, JOHAN 1735-1810. Several portraits of subjects with rod and tackle, engraved.

WALTER DENDY SADLER RBA: An angler on a riverside path. *Oil on canvas, 29¼ × 17¼ in.; signed and dated 1880.*

Appendix I

A list of known fishing tackle retailers and manufacturers from the last 350 years. ● denotes those companies who were also gunsmiths.

Found'd	Name	Address	Reference Dates
1745	Adlington & Hutchinson	Kendal, Cumberland	
	Thomas Aldred	126 Oxford St/58 King William St	1860–84
1819	W. H. Alfred & Sons	54 Moorgate St/41 Coleman St	c1880. Also at 20 Moorgate St
1803	S. Allcock & Co	Redditch	
	Edward Allen	198 Oxford St	1848, 1856
	Fred Allies	No. 8 Foregate St, Worcester	1861
	Mrs Mary Allort	41 Bethnal Green Rd, London	1867
	Anderson Archibald	71 Long Acre	1860
	R. Anderson	101 Prince St, Edinburgh	1851–90. Also at Dunkeld
	T. L. Andrews	High St, Chippingham	1892
	Armstrong & Co	113 Northumberland St, Newcastle-upon-Tyne	1909
	C. Armstrong	The Golden Perch, 178B Oxford St	1875
1790	Bambridge	Eaton	
	Henry Bancombe	No. 2A Victoria Rd, Holloway	c1880
	M. Barns	St Swithins Sq, Lincoln	
	Benjamin Barth	32 Cockspur St, London	
	Bartholemew	4 Crooked Lane, London	
1750	William Bartleet & Sons	Abbey Mills, Redditch/53 Gresham St	1890
	Bazin (John)	8 Duncan Place, London Fields	c1840
	Bazin	4 Church Place, Piccadilly	1840
	R. Snowden Beal	1 & 3 Station Rd.	1880
1825	J. Bernard & Son	4 & 5 Church Place, Jermyn St. London	
	Henry Bew	19 Nengate St, London	c1830
	John Billington	93 Chalton St, Somerstown	1840
	William Blacker	54 Dean St, Soho, London	c1840
	W. Blacklaws & Son	Kincardie, Aberdeenshire	1890
	J. R. Bolton	147 Northumberland St, Newcastle	1880
	Thomas Bond & Son	62 Cannon St, London	1840
1830	Alfred Booker & Co	Midland Works, Redditch	1890
	Bowden (Jno) Acton Co	14 Wood St, Cheapside, London	1830
	Davison & Bowness	33 Bell Yard, London	1809
1697	Bowness Bowness Bowness & Son	12–14 Bell Yard, London	
	Chevalier & Bowness	12 Bell Yard, London	1809
	George Bowness Jnr.	14 Bell Yard, London	
1811	● Jos. Braddell & Son	Castle Place, Castle Chambers, Belfast	1890
	William Brailsford	Hyson Green, Nottingham	
	Edward Brander	27 Wormwood St, Bishopsgate	c1840
	Charles Brandon	Nr The Swan, Golding Lane, London	1653
	Brough, Nicholson & Hall	Leek, Staffs.	c1890
	Sarah Brown	14 Mile End Rd, London	1830
	Will Brown	at The Sign of the Fish, Drury lane, London	
	William Brown	64 George St, Aberdeen	c1890
1881	Messrs Bulmer & Co	62 Wandsworth Rd, London	1890
	James L. Bullock	Regent House, King St, Clitheroe	1918
	J. Burron	16 Fishgate, Preston, Lincs	c1890
	G. Bustin	86 Magdelen Rd, Oxford	1923
	M. Carswell & Co	90 Mitchell St, Glasgow	1895
	Frank Carle		See W. S. Judd
1726	A. Carter & Co	137 St Johns St, London/1–3 Roseberry Ave, London	1726–1900
c1900	Carter & Peek		1900–12

Found'd	Name	Address	Reference Dates
	Cave, Robert	5 Oakley St, Lambeth, London	1848
	Cheek (Jno)	52 Strand, London	1839–48
	J. Cheek	132 Oxford St, London	1848–60
	John Cheshire & William Busilk	at The Angler and the Trout, Crooked Lane, London	c1730
1739	Samuel Chevalier		1739–1809 See Bowness
	Joseph Clark	11 St Johns Lane, London	1839–67
	Charles Clark	11 Compton St, London	1848
1770	● Cogswell and Harrison	168 Piccadilly, London & Exeter	1770–1982
	Thomas Clough & Co	51 High St, Kings Lynn	1923
	The Complete Angler	30/32 Worcester St, Birmingham	1930
	T. Courtney	Kilarney	1895
1850	J. Carlick		
	Creed (Ebenezer)	33 Wilderness Rd, Goswell St, London	1839–49
	Crofts (William)	47 Holywell Lane, Shoreditch, London	1867
	C. Crowshaw's Fishing Tackle Warehouse	36 The Pavement, York	c1800
1857	W. J. Cummins	Bishop Auckland, Co. Durham	1857–1909
	Cureton Jr.	9 Bull Alley, Lombard St, London	1839–67/1856 114 Snows Fields, Bermondsey
	Davis (Edmund)	12 Lower St, Islington, London	1839–67
1800	Benjamin Davis & Sons	Studley	
	Dawson (Edward)	33 Bell Yard, Temple Yard, London	1860/1867 Dawson & Bowness at same address
	Miss L. Davison	158 Stone St, Newcastle-on-Tyne	1909 Fly maker who had been working at J. R. Bolton for 10 years.
	Denton (Thomas)		See John Ramsden
	Dicks (Mrs E.)	112 St Johns Rd, Hoxton	1867
	Digings (Ann)	37 Gibson St, Lambeth, London	1839–48
	H. Dishley & Co	Leek, Staffordshire	1892
	Dixon (Hezekiah)	172 Fenchurch St, London	1848
	R. Dillon	78 Victoria Rd, Kentish Town, London	1896
	W. Dobson	West Thurston, Felton	1896
	● Dougall J. D.	Glasgow	1830–late 1800s
	Dowsett AC	10 York Buildings, Hastings, Sussex	1896
	Dunhill	125–127 Euston Rd, London	1895
	James Dyson & Co	Lincoln Works, Redditch	1892
	Eaton & Bernard	Edinburgh	1860
c1695	Eaton & Deller	6/7 Crooked lane, London	1839–95 and 1 Bury St, St James, London
	Eaton (George James)	Starkhomes, Matlock, Derbyshire	1880 Fly Tyer
	Edmunds (William)	15 East Rd/City Rd, London	1848–67
	J. Enright & Son	Castleconnell	1900 Fly rods
	Evatt (Abraham)	6 Warwick St, Golden Sq, London	1839–48
1840	C. Farlow & Co Ltd	221 Strand/10 Charles St/11 Phantom St, London	1840
	Farlow (John K.)	5 Crooked Lane/King William St, London	1848–73
	Fernandes (Marco)	2 Devonshire Sq, London	1867
c1653	Fletcher (Oliver)	at The Sign of the 3 Trouts, St Pauls	1653–97 shop owned by Will Brown
	Flint (John)	17 Essex Quay, Dublin	1861
	Ford (Thomas)	Lincoln, Lincs	1881
	Forrest & Sons	Kelso & 24 Thomas St/Oxford St, London	1860
1763	Foster Bros	Ashbourne, Derbyshire/St Johns Rd, London	1833/1933
	Fox (Mr)	Sheffield	1838
	Gardener W.	58 Goswell St, London	1848
	Garden (William)	122 Union St, Aberdeen	1895
	Gaynor & Son	4 Bridge St, Richmond-upon-Thames	c1883, 1915
	Gee (W)	19 Little St/Andrew St, London	1867
1695	Gillett (John)	115 Fetter Lane, Fleet St, London	c1695–1912
	Gould (Alfred)	268A Oxford St, London	1861–67
	Gowland & Co	3–4 Crooked Lane, London	1856–78
	Granville (George)	St Martin in the Fields, London	c1790
	Greene (C. J.)	54 London St, Norwich	1882
	Gregory (S.)	opposite St Clements Curch in the Strand	1773
	W. Guise & Sons	Redditch	1892
	Jemmy Hall	opposite Queens Head, Twickenham	1801
1837	W. T. Hancock & Co	308 High St, Holborn/4 Pall Mall, St James, London	1837–95 became Hancock & Watson

Found'd	Name	Address	Reference Dates
1872	Hardy Bros	Alnwick & 61 Pall Mall, London	1872 to date
1803	R. Harrison, Bartleet & Co	Metropolitan Works, Redditch	1803–92 See Bartleet
	W. Hayes & Son	63 Patrick St, Cork	1890–1915
	Jim Hearnes	Ballina, Co Mayo	1883–1915 Successor to Pat Hearnes
1857	Mr Reuben Heaton	161/165 Upper Hospital St, Birmingham	1857–92 Fine reel makers, wholesale only
1770	Hearder	Union St, Plymouth	c1900–15
	John Herro	The Fish and Crown, Bell Yard, London	c1734 Became Onesimus Ustonson
	Mr John Higginbotham	91 The Strand, London	c1770–1801 Formerly at the Complete Angler, 7 Holborn Bars
	Henry Hitchenman	64 Skinner St, Bishopsgate, London	1839
1815	George Hinton	Fare St, Taunton	1815–1915
	John Hobb	at the Sign of the George, behind the mews, by Charing Cross, London	1657 (Thomas Barber quotes him as the best rod maker)
1837	J. F. Hogg	79 Princes St, Edinburgh	1837–74 about 1861 became Mrs F. Hogg, 19 Princes St
	Holbrow	40 Duke St, St James, London	1880–1912 prior to 1880 in Jermyn St
	Hollamby (Benjamin)	24 Francis St, Twickenham	1867
	Geo Holland	29 The Square, Winchester	1888–95
	Holmes (Charles) Jon	2 Sydney Alley, Leicester Sq, London	1839–48 Formerly at 123 Fetter Lane (1856, 115 Fetter Lane)
1815	Holroyd J. S.	19 Fish Sheet Hill	1839–1900 From about 1848 at 59 Grayschurch St
	Homer (W. F.)	105 Wood Grange Rd, Forest Gate	1923
	Robert Hopkins	at the Sign of the Salmon, Bell Yard, Temple Bar	1700
	Charles Hutchinson	43 Strickland Gate, Kendal	
1745	P. Hutchinson & Son	43 Strickland Gate, Kendal	1909 Formerly Adlington & Hutchinson
	George Hutchinson, Turner	at Amberly Trout, Snow Hill, London	c1762
	Jacobs (G.)	32 Cockspur St, London	1865 Formerly Benjamin Barth
1844	W. M. James & Co	Criterion Works, Redditch	1844–92 Successor to H. James, N. Heath & Sons
	Messrs James, Jones & Co	111 Jermyn St, St James, London	1848–67 Successor to J. Jones (below)
	J. Jones	Princes St, Leicester Sq, London	1839–48
	Henry Joy	6 Opera Arcade, Pall Mall, London	1848–67
	W. S. Judd	33 Anlaby Rd, Hull	1923 Formerly Frank Carle
	Kenning (George)	4 Little Britain, London	1867
	Kennell (Charles)	98 St John St, London	1867
	Kerry E.	Marten, Sinnington, Yorks	1900
	King (Richard)	75 Cheapside, London	1848
	A. C. Kirby	23 Wide Bargate, Boston, Lincs	1923
c1655	Kirby (Mr Charles)	Globe Court, Hays Alley, Shoe Lane, Millyard	1655–1706 The best hook maker of Britain
	Kitchingham (Alfred)	37 Somerset Place, Hoxton	1867
	Mary Knight & Son	The Old Complete Angler, Crooked Lane	1760
	Laing	Aberdeen	1900
	Langs	5 Hanover St, Edinburgh	1858
	The Light Casting Reel Co	53 Market St, Bradford	1911 The Illingworth Reel
	D. W. Lindley	54 Victoria St, Crewe	1923
	W. M. Lister & Sons	Newcastle-on-Tyne	
c1820	G. Little & Co	15 Fetter Lane, Holborn, London	c1820–1923 Good reel maker, first to use aluminium c1887
	Bartholomew Lowe	at The Golden Fish, opposite Wych St	1762
	Samuel Lowkes	Upper Parliament St, Nottingham	1880
	Lucas & Walsh	45A Market St, Manchester	1884
	Macgowan (John)	7 Bruton St, New Bond St, London	1867
	R. J. Mack	Felton	1909
	Macpherson	Southampton	1900
	Herbert Magmar	16 Charles St, Mayfair, London	Early crank handle reel c1810
	G. Main	45 Jermyn St, London	
1875	P. D. Malloch	Scott St, Perth	
	Manchester Spring Co		1879
	March (J. N. O.)	118 Chancery Lane, London	1839
	James March	Waterloo Rd then 5 Great Charlotte St, Blackfriars & also 12 Webber St, London	1833–53
	John Margrave	at the sign of The Three Trouts, St Pauls, London	1657 Formerly Mr Oliver Fletcher

Found'd	Name	Address	Reference Dates
	John Martin	4 Belvedere, Cambridge Rd, London	
1778	●Alex Martin	Glasgow	1778 to date
	J. W. Martin	24 Northgate, Newark-on-Trent	1882–1907
	Martin & Penshaw & Co	24 Northgate, Newark-on-Trent	1892
	S. & E. G. Meseena	94 Clapton Road, London	later at 16 Guy St, Leamington Spa
	The Midland Rod Co	55 Worcester St, Birmingham	1923
c1899	J. E. Miller	New Station St, Leeds	1899–1909 (late of Francis M. Walbran
	●Henry Monk	77 Foregate St, Chester	1923
	Alfred Merriss	Redditch	1892
	J. B. Moscrop	25 Market Place, Manchester	1895
	Muirson J. T.	7 Upper King St, Bloomsbury & 36 Red Lion St, Holborn, London	
1848	Murton	Market St, Newcastle-on-Tyne	1900
	Henry A. Murton	8/10 Grange St, Newcastle-on-Tyne/ 27 Fawcett St, Sunderland	1909
	Mcfee (James)	30 Tabernacle Walk	1839
	J. McGowan	London	
	McKiernan (James)	15 St John's Lane, London & 7 Albion Place, Clerkenwell, London	1807
1763	Ogden Smiths	62 St James' St, London	
	Mr J. Ogden Smith	12 Park Road Villas, Norbiton	1895
	James Ogden	28 Winchcomb St, Cheltenham	1861–95
	Ogden & Scotford	19 Leicester Sq, London and Cheltenham	1888 Mrs James Ogden at 25 Crayford Rd, London
1825	O'Handley & Co (R. P. Frost)	48 Victoria St & Temple St, Bristol	c1900
	O'Shaughessey	of Limerick	1834–40
	Page (Jno)	118 Chancery Lane, London	1839
1830	●Pape (W. R.)	11 Collingwood St, Newcastle-upon-Tyne/ 29 Fawcett St, Sunderland	1830–1909
	E. Paton	Perth	
1831	Joshua Peach	of Derby	Reel maker
1837	J. Peek & Son	40 Grays Inn Rd, London	1837–1937 See also Carter & Peek 1588
	Stephen Penistone	The Sign of the Fish, Drury Lane, London	1756–72
	Phin	Edinburgh	
	J. Pickersgill	33 Rydall St, Holbeck, Leeds	1900
	Plucknett (Mrs)	45 Amelia St, Walworth Rd, London	1848
	M. Porritt	Stockton-on-Tees	1883
	Polden (Mrs)	29 Castle St, Leicester Sq, London	
	William Powell	Birmingham	1802 to date
	Purdon (Jno)	96 Wood St, London	1839
	Quarrier (Mrs Elizabeth)	17 Little Grays Inn Lane, London	1867
	R. Ramsbottom	81 Market St, Manchester	1895
	John Ramsden	Lightcliffs, Nr Halifax, Yorks	1756 A descendant of Thomas Denton, hook maker
1845	Redpath & Co	Kelso on Tweed, Scotland	1845–95
	Reynolds & Johnson	69 High Holborn, London	1867
1894	Frank Rhodes	Bar Street, Scarborough	1894–1915
1812	●Westley Richards	24 Bennetts Hill, Birmingham	1812 to date
	John R. Richardson	Kingston-on-Thames	1891
	W. M. Richmond	Eastgate St, Chester	
1675	John Rimmer & Sons	Alcester	1892
	W. F. F. Robertson	16 Market Place, Hexham on Tyne	1883
	John Robertson	c/o Grant Bros, 142 St James St, Edinburgh	1861
	William Robertson	27 Wellington St, Glasgow	1899
	M. Roberts	82/84 High St, Bala, Wales	1715 Established by G. Jones. first tackle business in Wales
	S. Roberts	10 Crooked Lane, London	c1800
	Roblow (Thos. Henry)	36 Upper Marylebone St, London	1839–67
	Rogan & Sons	Ballyshannon	c1883–1918
	Rowe	of Barnstaple	1840
	A. J. Rudd	Norwich Angler	Largest & best show of tackle at the 1894 Norwich Exhibition
1797	W. H. Ryder	Isaak Walton Works, Birmingham	1797–1892
	Mr Ryder	48 Ellis St, Birmingham	1879
	W. Sample	Amble	

Found'd	Name	Address	Reference Dates
	Sanderson (John)	10 Blackfriars Rd, London	1848
	Sarah Sandon	at the sign of the Complete Angler, Crooked Lane, London	Early 1700s–1760 Became Mary Knight & Son, later H. Stone & Iversen
1854	T. Shakespeare	9 Market St, Wolverhampton	1854–1923
	Silverlock, R.A.E, Co	51 Birdhurst Rise, South Croydon	1892
	Sims	44c Blackett St, Newcastle	1909
	David Slater	Newark on Trent & 9–10 Portland St, London	1852–82
	John Smail	14 Bridge St, Morepeth	
	Albert Smith	Dominion Works, Redditch	1912–33
	Smith	67 Wood St, & 1 Sherborne Lane	1845
	Smith	Bridge House, Richmond	1848
	J. F. Smythe Ltd	Darlington	1915
	Sneath (Charles)	11 Compton St, Clerkenwell, London	1839
	John Souch	at the sign of the Golden Salmon & Spectacles on Old London Bridge	1730 Wholesaler & Exporter
	J. Soulsby	Rothbury	1909
	Sowerbutts T. H.	3 Blossom Terrace, London	1867
	Mr Spalding	Bridge House, Richmond	1860
	Strachan (James)	22 Charlotte St, Fitzroy Sq, London	1867
	Stephens (Timothy)	7 Tottenham Ct Rd, London	1839
	R. C. Steven	West St, Berwick on Tweed	1853
	H. Stone & C. Iversen	at the Complete Angler, 13 Crooked Lane, London	See S. Sandon and also Stone (Harry)
c1890	J. Storer	13 Munk Park St, Coventry	1890–1923
	Henry Swann	of Langholm, North Britain	1816
	T. Taylor (R. W. Palmer)	69 Hazelbridge Rd, Hornsey Rise, London	1892
	Tennant (Frederick)	13 Broad Court, Bow St, London	1867
	Tennant (William M.)	6 Holywell Lane, London	1867
	W. A. G. Thicknesse	15 Piccadilly Arcade, London	1915
	Geo. H. Thompson	98 Great Thornton St, Hull	1923
	W. Thompson	22 George Strewt, Thornaby-on-Tees	1933 Tackle dealer
c1853	Walter Thompson	20 Scotland St, Sheffield	1853–88
	Turpin (Henry)	124 St John St, London	1848
	Thomas Tyson	Post Office, Renishaw, Nr Chesterfield	1888
	Onesimus Ustonson	No. 48 Bell Yard, Temple Bar, London	1760–93 He took over from John Herro about 1734
	Ustonson (Maria)	204 Fleet St, London	1830–49
	Ustonson & Peters	No. 48 Bell Yard, Temple Bar, London	1849
	Vieweg (Frances)	249 Old Kent Rd, London	1861
1899	Francis M. Walbran	19 New Station St, Leeds	c1899 Became J. E. Miller
	Walbrahan Ltd	38A Wellington St, Leeds	
1900	J. J. S. Walker Bampton	Northern Rd, Alnwick & Reelword	1900
	Ward (Richard)	Wellington St, Goswell St, London	1839
1830	J. Warner & Sons	Hewell Works, Redditch	1830–1911
1837	Watson & Hancock	308 High Holborn, London	1837–87 in 1882 Became W. Watson & Sons
	George Webster	The Fish, Chiswell St, Nr Moorfields, London	c1770
	Weekes & Son	27 Essex Quay, Dublin	1880
1860	Richard Wheatley & Son	30 Hockley St & 93 Spencer St, Birmingham	1860–1890
	Henry Whilty	15 Basult St, Liverpool	1819
	White Bros	Omagh, Ireland	1909
	Williams T.	26A Upper York St, Bryanston Sq, London	1867
	Charles D. Williams & Co	Belfast	1892
	Williams (Frederick)	13 Broadcourt, Bow St, London	1867 in 1887 moved to 110 Great Queen St, London
	Willis (John Jno)	120 Charing Lane, London	1839
	A. & G. Wilsons	34 Primrose St, Edinburgh	1858 Fishing Tackle Store
	W. Woodfield & Sons	Redditch	1867–92
	James Wright	Sprouston, Kelso, Perth	1860–83
	Charles Wright	376 Strand, London	1861–67
	Mr Richard Wyres & Mr Charles Swan	Redditch	1838 One of the best hook makers
	Alfred Young	174B Oxford St, London (The Golden Perch)	1878–83 Formerly at 402 Oxford St, London See also C. Armstrong

Appendix II

Hardy Reels and their dates of commencement of production and when discontinued, together with numbers of some of the reels whose production was confined to the period 1925 to 1939, taken from the Hardy Production Book for that period, the previous records having been destroyed during World War II:

Reel	Production dates	Quantity produced
Bronzed Gunmetal	1880-1921	
Nottingham Plain	1890-1920	
Perfect	1890-1966	
Ocean Reel	1894-1911	
The Field	1897-1907	
Farne	1897-1904	
Silex	1897-1911	
Nottingham – Silex Action	1899-1911	
Uniqua Mk.1 Trout	1903-1920	
Bougle	1903-1939	
Little Silex Tournament	1905-1911	
Special Perfect	1905-1939	
Farne Ebona	1905-1910	
Longstone, Ebona and Metal	1905-1959	
Ocean Ebona	1905-1910	
Megstone	1905-1927	
Perfect Silent Check	1908-1910	
Uniqua Salmon	1909-1959	
St George	1911-1983	
Coquet Sea Reel	1911-1921	
Silent No.2	1911-1922	
New Farne No.1, No.2, No.3	1911-1927	
New Ocean	1911-1911	
Nottingham Lever Action	1912-1921	
Silex No.2 Patent Surf Reel	1912-1913	
Eureka	1913-1955	
Sea Silex	1914-1959	
St George Silent Check	1920-1926	
St George Salmon 4½in.	1920-1924	
Tuna	1921-1922	
Silex No.2 Silent Wind	1921-1921	
Uniqua Mk.2 Trout	1921-1959	
St John (originally made for J.J.Hardy)	1923	
USA Fly Reel (radio silent variable brake)	1923-1923	
Silex Major	1923-1952	
Natal Surf	1923-1948	
Silex Minor	1923-1923	
Triumph	1923-1928	
Sunbeam	1924-1956	
J.J.Hardy's Silex	1924-1928	114
Silex Multiplier	1924-1939	
Fortuna Big Game Reel	1924-1956	
Auxiliary Brake 3½in. – Uniqua, Silex and Perfect	1925-1929	
Filey	1925-1939	302

Reel	Production dates	Quantity produced
Fortuna Fly - 3½in.	1925-1939	77
4¼in.		58
5in.		70
Alma 4in.	1926-1935	4
4¾in.		18
5¼in.		23
5¾in.		47
7in.		5
Hardy Zane Grey	1928-1957	
St George Multiplier – 3⅜in.	1928-1939	349
3¾in.		142
St George Junior – 2⁹⁄₁₆in.	1928-1964	
Super Silex	1928-1953	
Special Longstone for Dorado	1928-1939	1
Davy	1930-1939	173
Tournament Revolving Drum	1931-1934	
Improved Farne	1931-1934	
South African Surf Casting	1931-1948	
Hardy-Decantelle Bait Casting	1931-1950	
Hardy-Willis Bottom Fishing Reel	1931-1939	535
Cascapedia Fly Reel – 1/0	1932-1939	113
2/0		36
3/0		39
4/0		26
Altex No.1	1932-1965	
Altex No.2	1932-1966	
Hardy-White-Wickham (the Production Book records only two made. They were priced at £37 10s)	1934-1939	2
The Barton Dry Fly Reel	1934-1939	109
President (as entered in Production Book)	1934-?	3
Finn de Lang	1937-?	65
Silex Rex - 3½in.	1935-1937	85
3¼in.		48
4¼in.		1
Altex No.3	1935-1963	
Lightweight Reel	1936-1964	
Hardex No.1	1937-1957	
Sea Altex	1937-1959	
Match Fisher's	1937-1939	
Triumph	1937-1951	
New Brunswick	1938-1939	
Hardy Jock Scott	1938-1952	
No.2 Hardex	1939-1959	
Elarex	1939-1964	
Goodwin	1940-1959	
L.R.H. Lightweight	1951	
Princess	1953-1959	
Silex Jewel	1954-1959	
Conquest	1955-1966	
Zenith	1958-1980	
Featherweight	1958	

Reel	Production dates
Taupo Perfect	1958-1964
Exalta	1958-1965
Hydra	1958-1967
Silex Superba	1960-1971
Flyweight	1961
Princess	1962
St Andrew	1962-1969
Gem	1962-1969
St Aidan	1964
Husky	1964-1969
No.4 to No.10	1969
Viscount 130,140,150	1969-1978
Longstone	1969
Marquess Salmon No.1 & No.2	1970
Marquess Multiplier	1971
Silex	1972
Featherweight Multiplier	1973-1979
L.R.H. Lightweight Multiplier	1974-1980
Princess Multiplier	1974-1980
Zenith Multiplier	1974-1980
Sunbeam 5/6, 6/7, 7/8, 8/9, 9/10	1978-1983
Perfect – reinforced	1978
Husky	1978-1980
Uniqua – reintroduced, new model	1981-1983
Viscount – reintroduced	1981-1983
Marquess Salmon No.3	1981
Marquess Salmon No.1, No.2, No.3 Silent	1982-1985
Viscount Silent	1982-1983
Prince 5/6, 7/8	1983
Zane Grey	1983
Golden Prince 5/6, 7/8	1984
Ocean Prince One	1984
Golden Prince 9/10, 11/12	1985
Ocean Prince Two	1985
Marquess 2/3	1985
Marquess Silent Check	1985

Extracts from the Hardy Production Book describing the company's manufacturing record between 1925 and 1939. The records for the preceding years have been destroyed but some figures for earlier years are included in the existing records.

	Fly reels	Silex & Sea reels, etc.	Total
1913	2678	1234	3912
1920	3422	1493	4915
1921	5689	1407	7096
1922	2852	1193	4045
1923	3036	941	3977
1924	3917	1446	5363
1925	4766	1592	6358
1925	4766	1592	6358
1926	6204	1396	7600
1927			8015
1928			7614
1929			8497
1930			8975
1931			4960

Index

Page numbers in *italic* refer to illustrations and captions

Abbey and Imbrie reel, 66
accessories, 89-110
Aelian, Claudius, 73
Aeriel reel, 55-7, *56*, 134
Ainge & Aldred, 29
Albert Victor, Prince, 114-15, 120
Aldred & Sons, 30
Alfred, Henry Jervis, *146*
Alken, Henry, 140-1, *142*
Allcock, Polycarp, 134
Allcock, Samuel, 134
Allcock's, 38, 57-8, 96
  Aeriel Fishing Reel, 55-7, 134
  catalogues, *132*, 134
  floats, 109
  rods, *132*
  Stanley reel, 58-60
Allen, John, *81*
Altex, 60
Andsell, Richard, 142
Archemedian reel, *43*
art, angling, 137-50
ash rods, 20, 24-5
auctions, 10

Baden-Powell, W., 115-16
Baker, C. Alma, 127
bamboo rods, 22, *22*, 28-34
Barker, Thomas, 37, 141
Barlow, Francis, 139
baskets, *108*, *109*, 110
bass plugs, 10
bass rods, 30
Bernard, J., 29
Bernes, Dame Juliana, 73, *74*
Bickerdyke line guide, *121*
Billinghurst reel, 50, 65
Blacker, William, 29, *81*
Blue Elver salmon fly, 76
Blue Grass reels, 64
blue mahoe rods, 26
boats, *93*
Boschen, William, 68
Bowness & Bowness, *39*, *84*
Bradford & Anthony, 30, 31
Bristow, Edmund, 141
Bronson, 68
Buckland, Frank, 147

cane rods, 22, *22*, 28-34
Carter, William, 68
Carter & Co., 50, 75, 96, 98, 103
catalogues, 128-36
Catskill rods, 31-2
China, reels, 38
Chippendale reels, *43*
Cholmondeley-Pennell, H., 32, 41,
  48-50, 66, 100, 101, 115
Clark, Andrew, 31, 64
Clarke, Henry, 114
Clinch, Douglas W., 48
Clinton, 65
clothes, 12-13
compendiums, *103*, *107*
Condor feathers, 76
Conroy, J.C., 64, *64*, 65
Conroy, Thomas, 68
Constable, John, 141
Cook, J.B., 64, *64*
Cooper, J., 147
Cope, Tome, 61
cork floats, *107*
Corta gut, 95
Cotman, John Sell, 141
Cox, David, 141
Cox, J.A., 68
Coxon, H., 55-6
Coxon Aeriel reel, *43*, 55-7, *56*
Cozzone, 67
creels, *100*, *108*, *109*, 110
Cummins, W.J., 51

dagane rods, 26
Dame Stoddard & Kendall, *32*
Daniel, *Rural Sports*, 16, 20, 23, 29,
  80, 89, 90, 96, 104-9
De Wint, Peter, 141
Devine Rainbow rod, 62
Devis, Arthur, 142
Dodd, Ashley, *84*
doone fly, 74
Dougal, J.D., 50
Dowagiac, 68
drawn gut, 98
dress, 12-13
Drew, Julius, 142
dryers:

lines, *90*, 98-9
  winders, 98-9
dyes, lines, 90-2
dying feather, 79-84

Eaton and Deller, 15, *39*, 49, *60*
elder rods, 20
Enright, John, 97
Erskine, J., 47

factories, 12, *30*, *94*
Fairy Catskills, 32
Farlow, J.K., 29
Farlow & Co., 49, *49*, 80, 84, *85*
  gaffs, 101
  Improved Landing Net, 101
feathers, fly tying, 76-9
Fisheries Exhibition 1887, 147
Fisheries Exhibition 1896, 44, 50, 75,
  97, 100-1, 134
Fisheries Exhibition 1900, 112
Fishing Gazette, 12, 128
flies, 73-6
  books, 103
  cabinets, *91*
  cases and boxes, *80*, *83*, *84*, 85-6,
    85, *86*, *103*
  dyes, 79-84
  feathers, 76-9
  hooks, 84
  materials, 76-9
  pouches and wallets, 84
  tools, 76, 77
floats, 103-10
Follett, 50, 65
Follett winch, *61*
Forrest & Sons, 79
Fowler, 65
Francis, Francis, 40
Frankland, Sir Robert, *142*
fur, fly tying, 76-9

gaff/priest, 101
gaffs, 101-2, *102*, *107*
Gibbs Patent Locking Lever, 46, 47
Gillet, C., 97-8
gimp lines, 98
Gladstone fly, 75

Granger, 34
Great Exhibition 1851, 29, 112
Great Fisheries Exhibition 1883, 32, 41, 50, 112
Green, E.A., 30
greenheart rods, 25, 26
Greville, Capt., 115
Grey, Secombe, 46
Grey, Zane, 68, *118*, 127
Griffiths, Sir Waldie, 100
gut lines, 92-8

hair, fly tying, 78
hair lines, 89-92
Hardie, Charles Martin, *142*
Hardy, Charles, 121
Hardy, Forster, 121
Hardy, John James, 112
Hardy, L.R.H., 114
Hardy, Robert, 121
Hardy, William, 111-12
Hardy's, 111-27
  Albert Victor rod, 120
  Alma, 127
  Altex reel, 127
  Bethune line winder, 99
  Bouglé reel, *122*, 12y
  C.C. de France rod, 113
  catalogues, *129*, 133
  Champion rod, 120
  Conquest reel, *122*
  creels, *108*, *109*
  Driver Perfection rod, 120
  Ebona reel, *122*
  Elarex reel, 127
  Eureka reel, 127
  Field reel, *121*
  fly books, 84
  fly boxes, *83*
  fly cabinets, 86, *91*
  Fortuna reel, 127
  Hardex, 60
  Hercules reel, 50, *122*
  H1 Regan rod, 120
  Houghton rod, 120
  Improved Y-Shaped Collapsing
    Landing Net, 100
  Jock Scott reel, *120*, 127
  Kelson rod, 115, 120
  landing nets, 100
  L.H.R. reels, 127
  line winders, *91*, *99*, *120*
  Longstone reel, *122*
  Marston Perfection rod, 120
  Nottingham reel, *121*
  Pennell rod, 120
  Perfect creel, *109*
  Perfect reel, *50*, *111*, *119*, 121-2, *121*, *122*, *123*, 127

Perfect Test rod, 120
Perfection rod, 120
priests, 103
Princess rod, 120
reels, 68, 121-7, *121*, *126*, *127*
Rhodesian Reels, 117
rings, *25*
rods, 22, 32-3, 112, *116*, 120
St George reel, *60*, 127
St John reel, *127*
Sea Silex reel, 127
seats, *91*
Silex reels, *122*, 127, *127*
        South African Surf Casting
Reels, 117
Sunbeam reel, 127
Super Silex reel, *122*
trophies, *138*
Uniqua reel, 127
Wallis reel, *122*
White-Wickham reel, 11
Zane Grey reels, 68, *119*, 127
Harrison, Mr, *103*
Harmsworth, Alfred C., 66-7
hazel rods, 16-20
Heaton, 48
Heddon, 34, 68, 72
Hemmingway rods, *28*
Hendryx Co., 71
Henshaw, James, 65
hickory rods, 25
hip briar rods, 29
Hippurus fly, 73
Holland, 79
holly rods, 20
hooks, 84
Horton, 72

Illingworth, A.H., 51
Illingworth reel, 51-5, *52*, *53*, *54*, *55*
Indiana reels,66

Johnson, George H., 116-17
Jones, J., *43*
Jones, William, *137*, 141
Jungle Cock feathers, 76

Keene, John Harrington, 24, *38*, 65, 81, 89, 92
Kelson, George, 32, 115
Kentucky Reel, 62-4
Kingston Bite Indicator, 110
Knott, W.A., 46
Krider, 64

lancewood rods, 26
landing nets, 99-101, *100*
Layman Pneumatic Boats, *93*
Leonard, Hiram Lewis, 31-4, 113, 134
lines, 89-98

dryers, *90*, 98-9
dyes, 90-2
gimp, 98
gut, 92-8
hair, 89-92
silk, 98-9
winders, 89-90, *90*, *91*,98-9, *120*
Luke, Charles H., 29
Lyson, Sir Daniel, 49

McLean, Thomas, *142*
Malloch, 45-8, *46*, *48*
  Casting Reel, 45, *45*
  Erskine Patent spinning reel, 45, 47, 51
  fly boxes, *84*
  Side Casting Reel, 51
  Sun and Planet reel, 47-8, *47*
Malloch, P.D., 45
Marston, R.B., 12, 120
Martin, Alexander, *54*
Martin's, 98
May, Princess, 120
mayflies, 75
Meek, B.F., 64
Meek, Jonathan Fleming, 64
Meek and Millam, 64
Meeks, 72
Meisselbach, A.E., *62*, 72
Mequiner, John, *141*
Millam, B.C., 64
Miller, J.E., *43*
Mills, William, 31, 33, 134, *134-5*
Mitchell, William, 29
Mitchell Henry reel, *59*
Moore Rapid, *43*
Moravian Piscatorial Society, 98
More, Mr, *54*
Morris, Thaddeus, 30
mountain ash rods, 20
Muller, William, *141*
multipliers, 40-1
Murphy, Charles, 30, *31*
Murton, Henry, 135-6

nets, landing, 99-101, *100*
Nottingham rod, 131
Nottingham winches, *41*, *42*, 44, *45*

Ogden and Scotford Fishing Bag, 110
Orford, Lord and Lady, 67
Orvis, Charles F., 34, 50, 65-6, 67, 113
Orvis Pennell Reel, 50
Orvis Trout Reel, 50, 66
Osborn, W., *107*

paintings, 137-46, *137-41*
Payne and Chippendale reels, *42*
Pennell reel, 48-50, *51*

Pflueger, 72
Phillippe, Samuel, 29
pirns, 39-40, *39*
Pollard, James, 141
priests, 102-3, *103*

Queen of the May Fly, 75
quill floats, 107-8

Rainbow reel, *62*
Ramsbottom, R., 92-5
Redditch, 84, *94*, 109
reels:
  American, 61-72
  British, 37-60
  Chinese, 38
  introduction, 23
Richardson, J.R., 75, 110
  Surbiton Bag, 110
Richardson, Mrs J.R., 75
rings:
  19th century, *24*, *25*
  introduction, 23
roach pole, 40
rods, 15-34
  17th century, 15-16
  18th century, 15-16
  19th century, 22ff.
  hollow butt ends, 22
  joints, 19, 112
  sectional, 16
  spikes, 22, *23*
  spliced joints, 19
  split cane, 22, *22*
  tops, 22
  walking-stick rods, *107*
  woods, 20, 24-8
Rolfe, Henry Leonidas, 146, 147
Rowe, J., 79

salmon rods, 20, 23, 30, 120
saltwater reels, 68
Scarborough reel, 45
Searl, 147
seats, *91*
sectional rods, 16
  joints, 19
  spliced joints, 19
Senior, William, *32*, 115
Shakespeare Co., 34, 71-2
Sharps, 19
Shipley, 64
shop signs, *130*
silk lines, 98-9
silkworm gut, 92-5
Skinner, Frederick, *43*
Slater, David, 12, 128-32
  Combination Reel, 44-5
  latch, *43*, 45
  reels, *43*, 44-5
  Scarborough reel, 45
Smith, John Raphael, *139*
Smith, Ogden, 75, 136
Smith & Wall, 41
Snyder, George, 62-3
Southbend, 34
Sparrow, W. Shaw, 137
spliced joints, rods, 19
split cane rods, 22, *22*, 28-34
Stark, James, 141
steelwood rods, 26
Stevens, James Alexander, 29
Surbiton Bag, 110
Sussex Piscatorial Society, 99

tackle compendiums, *103*, *107*
taxidermy, 146-7
Thompson, *91*
Thread Line Spinning Reel, 51

Ticehurst, Robert, 117
tools, fly tying, 76, 77
trophies, *138*, 146-7
trout rods, 20
Turner, Charles, *142*
Turner, J.M.W., 141
Twiti, Guillaume, 73

Ustonson, Onesimus, *49*

Valentine reel, 48
varnish, 19, 21
vices, fly tying, 76, 77, *91*
Vom Hofe, Celebrated reel, 66
  Peerless reel, 65
  Perfection reel, 65
  Restigouche reel, 65
  Tibique reel, 65
Vom Hofe, Edward, 34, *65*
Vom Hofe, Julius, *63*, 67, 68
Vulterine Guinea Fowl feathers, 76

walking-stick rods, *107*
Walton, Izaac, 16, 37, 76-8, 110
washaba rods, 26
Weeger, Emil, 98
Wells, Walter, 98
Williams, *85*, 100
winders, line, 89-90, *90*, *91*, *120*
Wood, Mr, 66-7
woods, for rods, 20, 24-8
wynches, 38

Yawman & Erbe, *71*
yew rods, 20

Zoffany, John, 142